HOW TO BE A BRILLIANT SPIRITUAL TEACHER

Margaret Merrison

ISBN 978-1-291-95460-9

CONTENTS

INTRODUCTION

How to Be a Brilliant Spiritual Teacher has been written by drawing on my 12 years' experience of teaching and running spiritual courses. I started by teaching reiki healing in 2002. I only had the guidance of my reiki master and was very nervous, to the point that most of my programmes finished early because I rushed through them, trying to get them over as soon as possible. Needless to say, this is not the way to run courses!

In 2003, I went on a three-week course in Wales to learn to teach about angels and ascension with Diana Cooper. This gave me so much more knowledge and confidence for spiritual teaching, as well as becoming really connected with angels and having an in-depth understanding of ascension. I am indebted to Diana Cooper for sharing her wisdom of good spiritual training, some, of which, is included in the following pages.

When I returned home, I could hardly wait to start teaching. A little while later I ran an angel day and really enjoyed it. Since then I have hosted a variety of spiritual courses and meetings on topics such as reiki, angels, ascension, unicorns, Lemurian planetary healing, spiritual beginners, angel healing practitioner, unicorn healing practitioner as well as courses held in conjunction with The Diana Cooper School (now The Diana Cooper Foundation) to instruct others how to teach specific spiritual courses.

While I was a principal teacher with The Diana Cooper School, I co-wrote some of the teaching manuals. One such manual is the *Foundation Manual* and some information that I wrote for this manual is included in *How to Be a Brilliant Spiritual Teacher*.

How to Be a Brilliant Spiritual Teacher provides the reader with information about spiritual teaching and can be applied with material from many different spiritual applications. As there is already a wealth of spiritual knowledge and many different belief systems, this book does not give you any subject matter, except some visualisations, meditations and activities that can be adapted to fit a number of situations. It is for you to add your teaching material and weave your unique energies and principles into your meetings.

If you wish to teach a certain subject that you are not familiar with, then you must study and connect with this energy before you can teach it.

How to Be a Brilliant Spiritual Teacher often refers to higher beings. This is so you can adapt your meetings or courses to teach about any member of the higher realms, be they spirit guides, angels, archangels, unicorns, ascended masters or any other higher being.

I hope that you will find the pleasure and fulfilment that I have had in helping others with their spiritual path. It is wonderful to watch somebody realising a spiritual truth or witnessing that moment when they connect with their higher being or sense spiritual energy for the very first time.

With love and blessings

Margaret Merrison
August 2014

CHAPTER ONE

BEING A LEADER

By the end of Chapter One you will:

- Know why you want to teach

- Understand the responsibilities of being a leader

- Be able to present yourself as a leader

- Recognise how to create the right impact with your voice

Why Do you Want to Teach?

Teaching others can be an enjoyable and rewarding experience. It is wonderful to see somebody's eyes light up as they resonate with a spiritual truth or recount 'seeing' a spiritual being in a meditation you have just led. The key to spiritual teaching is to show others the path and then guide them to walk it for themselves.

There are a number of things you need to clarify for yourself before you begin to teach others. First, ask yourself: "Why do I want to teach?" Spend some time thinking deeply about this question, because it will set the precedent for your teaching career. However, only you are able to answer it. For some people, wanting to teach others is a compelling desire to pass on their knowledge; for others, people may have naturally followed them; or some individuals simply have an inner knowing that this is what they are meant to be doing in this life. Whatever your reasons, it will probably be part of your destined life plan.

The next question to ask yourself is: "What messages or principles do I want to convey aside from my course material?" Do you want to tell people about your understandings of reincarnation, spiritual laws, subtle energies, spirits etc? Spiritual teaching is open to many different belief systems. When teaching the higher realms nothing is black and white. You cannot say that your beliefs are better than anybody else's, so be open to other people's convictions.

Now ask yourself: "What do I want to teach?" You probably have some idea of this already; but, whatever your subject matter, you must know it inside out and back to front, not only what you are actually going to teach in your courses, but much more, because of the inevitable questions that will be asked.

You now need to think about what attributes you have that will help you to teach others. This is not necessarily always being in the limelight or the life and soul of parties. Shy people often make brilliant spiritual teachers, usually because they have a passion and have thought deeply about their subject matter, and this is conveyed to their students. Teaching may be in your family (spiritual or mainstream), and certain family members may be used to leading others, which may be passed onto you. You may be good at speaking, leading meditations or able to convey information well. Also think about the tones of your voice, how you deal with people, your knowledge of the subject, your ability to retain information and your guidance from your higher beings. Do not worry if you do not feel you have many teaching attributes – you probably have more than you think. The key ingredient is to have enthusiasm for your subject matter, as this will give others the motivation to learn.

You as a Leader

Being a leader can be a big responsibility. Others may want to copy you or be like you, so you need to be careful with the words that you use and how you act. On the flip side, if somebody does not resonate with you or what you represent and there will inevitably be some, they will be critical of you, your exploits and achievements. Either way, you must always present yourself as a good, compassionate, truthful leader and the best way to do this is to be a good, compassionate, truthful person. Being on your spiritual path makes this easier, so adhere to the principles of your spiritual beliefs.

As a guide, always:

- Say only good, positive words.

- Think good, positive thoughts as much as possible. This can be difficult when living in the physical world, but just realising when your thoughts are not as pure as you would like will help you to connect with the higher realms.

- Do good, positive deeds and nothing that will harm anybody, any animal, any being or any thing.

- Have only good, positive emotions. Again, as we are human, this can be difficult at times, but try to consciously be as positive as possible.

Presenting yourself as a Leader

Always speak your truth, and if you do not believe in something, say so. If you do not know something, again, say so, because if you pretend or bluff your way it will show, and your students will not respect you or your work. By speaking your truth, others will acknowledge that you are faithful to your beliefs, as well as being open and frank, so they will hold you in high esteem.

If somebody in your meeting has different convictions, respect them and their beliefs and do not belittle them. We are all different and have had different physical as well as spiritual upbringings in this and previous lives. As a result, every one of us is different physically, emotionally, mentally and spiritually.

Throughout your daily life, and especially on the days that you are teaching, try to have a balanced approach. This means being as grounded and protected as you can be. Grounding and protection will be explained in Chapter Three: *Good Spiritual Teaching Practice*. You also need to be in connection with the energies and beings that you resonate with, especially those you are going to work with when teaching.

To help with a balanced lifestyle:

- Practise daily meditation. See Chapter Four: *How to Lead a Visualisation or Meditation* for further information on meditation.

- Practise daily breathing exercises. Some breathing exercises are explained in the *Leading Meditations* section in Chapter Four.

- Spend time in nature every day to connect with the natural world. Go to a garden, the countryside, a park, a forest or beside the sea and use all of your senses. For example, touch a leaf or grain of sand; smell the aromas around you; listen to the wind, the birds, the sea and other sounds; and also look around and take in all the beauty that surrounds you.

- Do gentle daily exercise, especially if you have a sedentary life style. However, if you have an active life, this is not needed. Listen to your body's needs and respect them.

- Eat natural, uncontaminated, food and drink, if you are not already doing so. To do this, reduce your intake of toxins by cutting out or drinking minimal amounts of tea, coffee, fizzy drinks and alcohol, and instead drink plenty of water (filtered preferably), herbal or fruit drinks. Try not to eat processed food, but plenty of fresh fruit and vegetables (preferably organic if you can get it, or thoroughly wash the fruit or vegetables if not). You can always ask your higher beings to help you make good food and drink choices that will nurture your body.

- See the beauty and good in everyone and everything. There is a spark of goodness in everybody, no matter what they may have done.

- Be grateful for all that you have and all that there is, not just material things, but family, friends, your students, the air that you breathe, your food and also your gifts, talents and qualities, e.g. generosity, calmness, happiness. It is good practice to do this every day, and it is especially beneficial to thank the higher beings for the events of your day and the lessons you have been given.

- Try not to expose yourself to negative energies, such as watching violent TV programmes or films or reading violent books or newspapers.

- If possible, keep away from negative people. These are people who hardly ever say anything positive about their circumstances or unconsciously take your higher energies. You know when somebody has taken your energy, because you feel drained and tired after being in their company. Protecting yourself usually stops this from happening.

- Stay away from buildings or places that give off an uncomfortable feeling, if you can. This is because there is stuck energy within the walls, which is the residue of negative events that have happened there in the past. If you live or work in such a building, cleanse it. Cleansing buildings and rooms is discussed in Chapter Two: *Your Teaching Environment*.

- Regularly cleanse your physical body by visualising all unwanted and unneeded energies, including toxins, travelling down your body, through your legs and leaving via your feet. Ask your higher beings to spiritually change these energies to positive vibrations while you visualise your body and its organs functioning perfectly.

- Regularly cleanse your aura by visualising any unwanted energies leaving, which usually appear as dull, murky colours in the aura, and see them changing to a positive white colour as they go. Then visualise your whole aura gleaming brightly with wonderful, radiant, pure colours.

- Do reflective writing. Buy or beautifully decorate a book in which you can write your thoughts. Write in it every day at about the same time so that it becomes a habit. Look back over your day. Notice how you have reacted to situations and how you feel about yourself or others, and then think and note how you may have reacted differently and what the outcome may have been if you had done so. If you feel you overreacted, try to respond in a more positive and calm way the next time a similar situation presents itself. As time progresses, look back over your book and see the wonderful changes in yourself. Reflective writing is especially important after you have been teaching, because it will help you to become a good leader.

Personal Preparation for Teaching
When you are preparing for your course or meeting:

- **Have the highest good of all in your heart**: Make sure you are teaching for all the right reasons. You may like to make a positive statement for your course or meeting. For example: "I run excellent, enjoyable courses with information and practical training of the highest standard to enable my participants to connect well with their higher beings for their highest and greatest good." Put your positive statement in your own words and, when you have made it, say it as many times as you can to yourself before your course, like an affirmation. Affirmations are positive statements made in the present tense which are said a number of times a day so that the meaning of the words sinks into the subconscious; consequently, it can make it happen.

- **Be yourself**: An important quality when it comes to teaching is to be yourself. Do not try to model yourself on anybody else, no matter how good you think they are, it simply will not work. You have special gifts, talents and skills which you should bring out when teaching. People will respect you and learn more if you teach in your own unique way.

- **Be professional**: To be professional, visualise how you would like to come across to your students and then act on it. Professional people do not gossip and do not discuss personal problems unless they are relevant to the course or meeting. If you do so, do it from a teaching perspective, not as you would if you were talking to a friend or a therapist.

- **Be your best**: Go to other courses and meetings to see how they are run. Note how you and others feel and then learn from it. Make a note of the parts that went well and think how you could improve the elements that were not so good. When you have run your own gatherings, do this for yourself in the same way as your reflective writing.

- **Prepare your meeting**: Make sure you are thoroughly prepared before you teach. For a few weeks before your gathering, prepare for it as explained in Chapter Seven: *Putting Together a Good Programme* and Chapter Eight: *Organisation and Administration*. Also, leave time to go over your course or meeting the day before, and if you know who is attending try to memorise names and remember some details about them.

- **Know your coursework**: Thoroughly know your subject matter by reading as many books as you can on your topic, and try to remember most of what you have read.

- **Practise encouragement**: You should always teach by encouraging others and not deriding them. People learn by being told they are doing well. Practise encouraging people in your everyday life with family, friends and colleagues.

- **Practise empathy**: Always try to understand others and sense their feelings, because then they will feel safe in your company and be able to open up. If you empathise with your students when you are teaching, it will help them to relax and they will learn more.

- **Dress**: When running your meetings and courses, dress appropriately and smartly with suitable colours for the subject you are conveying. You need people to be able to identify with you, and if they are put off by the way that you dress they may not learn as much as they otherwise would. It can be beneficial to set aside some clothes just for teaching, because when you put them on it will put you in your teaching mode and give you confidence. Also, do not wear excessive perfume or after shave, or, better still, do not wear any at all, because what smells great for you may not be good for others.

- **You are not alone**: Use your own spiritual network of guides, angels or whoever you believe in for help and guidance.

Preparing your Voice

One of your most important assets when teaching is your voice. A calm, pleasant, confident voice, where every word can be heard from anywhere in the room, can have a positive, relaxing impact on your students. You need to learn the skills of using your breathing, as well as the volume, tones and pace of your voice, to ensure your speech is clear and interesting and has the desired impact.

Breathing correctly helps to relax the chest and throat muscles as well as produce volume and prevent fading at the end of sentences. Deep voice tones help people to relax, and if you talk slowly and with emphasis it gives words importance. High-pitched voices can lift people and help to connect them with the higher realms, as long as what is said is not spoken too quickly. If you speak too quickly in a high pitched voice it will make you come across as being unsure and unconfident.

When you first run your courses or meetings you will need to practise changing the tone and pace of your voice to avoid sounding nervous and self-conscious, because when we are worried and anxious we tend to tense up, breathe shallowly, raise our voice tones and speak quickly, making our words difficult to understand.

To follow are some exercises to help you with your speaking voice, they will: aid relaxation, assist with breathing correctly, develop voice tones, assist with articulation and help with pace. Try doing them two or three times everyday, especially just before a course or meeting. However, do not do them for long periods, and if your voice tires or your throat feels dry or sore make sure that you stop, as you will be overworking your throat. Also, if any exercise gives you pain or discomfort it is important that you stop immediately.

To Relax the Body
Throughout this exercise, focus on removing tension from your muscles, especially in the upper body.

- Stand up straight, stretch your arms up and breathe in.

- On the out breath, bend forwards at the waist as far as is comfortable while uttering an "aah" sound.

- Lift and drop your shoulders three times, breathing in while lifting and breathing out whilst dropping.

- Shake your shoulders for about 10 seconds.

- Shake your body for about 10 seconds.

- Repeat all the above three to five times.

To Relax the Throat and Voice
Throughout this exercise hum gently from deep in your chest, not your throat.

- Stand or sit, making sure that you are comfortable.

- Place your hands on your throat muscles and gently massage them for about 30 seconds.

- Yawn and really stretch your mouth for about 10 seconds.

- With your jaw dropped, move it from side to side for about 10 seconds.

- Close your lips keeping a loose jaw, and continue humming from your chest for about 10 seconds.

- Repeat the above process three to five times.

To Improve Confidence, Voice Volume and Tone

To gain more confidence, stand up straight, without slouching, because slouching restricts the breath and also makes you feel and sound less confident. Good deep breathing leads to a good voice tone. You should aim to speak from the bottom of your lungs by pushing the air and your voice upwards using the diaphragm muscles, which are at the bottom of your ribs and control your breathing. To demonstrate this for yourself, stand in a relaxed position, without slouching. Put your hands at the bottom of your rib cage and first breathe into your upper chest. Next, breathe deeply into your lower ribs and notice, with the movement of your hands, how much more air is moved.

As you do these exercises your diaphragm muscles will be strengthened. These exercises should be done standing in a comfortable, upright, confident position. It is especially beneficial to do them outside in clean, fresh air.

- Exhale every last drop of air from your lungs and then inhale slowly and evenly. Repeat three times. If you feel faint or giddy stop immediately, breathe normally and sit or lie down.

- Exhale in the usual way and then inhale to normal capacity and hold it for at least 10 seconds. Repeat twice more and see how long you can comfortably hold your breath each time. The more this is practised over time, the longer you will be able to hold your breath, but only repeat a maximum of three times per session.

- Keeping your lips closed, laugh through your nose for 30 seconds. This will help you to control your breathing. Repeat three to five times.

- Take a deep breath in and, as you exhale, count slowly aloud from 1 to 6 before inhaling. Make sure that you pronounce each number properly. Repeat, but count slowly from 1 to 8 on exhalation. Repeat as many times as is comfortable, counting two more numbers each time.

To Improve Articulation
It is no good having a strong melodic voice if people cannot understand the words you are saying. The best ways to improve articulation are to increase the flexibility of the lips and tongue.

To exercise the lips:
- Tightly pucker your lips.

- Open your lips as wide as possible.

- Repeat the above 10 times, as quickly as possible, without compromising maximum mouth movement.

To exercise the tongue: There are some well-known tongue twisters, which sound funny when they are not articulated as intended. Say each tongue twister five times, first slowly and then get faster each time making sure that every word is perfectly formed.

Red lorry, yellow lorry.

I saw Esau sitting on a seesaw.

I scream, you scream, we all scream for ice cream.

Can you can a can as a canner can can a can?

One-one was a racehorse
Two-two was one too
One-one won one race and
Two-two won one too.

Peter Piper picked a peck of pickled peppers.
Did Peter Piper pick a peck of pickled peppers?
If Peter Piper picked a peck of pickled peppers,
Where's the peck of pickled peppers Peter Piper picked?

She sells sea-shells by the seashore.
The shells she sells are surely seashells.
So if she sells shells on the seashore,
I'm sure she sells seashore shells.

To Practise Using Tone and Emphasis

You need to use different tones to make your speech interesting. Try listening to the pitches and word emphasis of others delivering information to gain an idea of what is needed, e.g. newsreaders on the television.

Practise saying the following sentence by changing your pitch according to the line beneath. For example, if the line goes up then raise your tone. Also, use emphasis, which is indicated by the bold words, by speaking slower. Do this five times.

"Many people come to my meetings, as I am a **brilliant**

spiritual teacher and leader"

Next, say it again five times, but this time lowering your pitch when the line goes up and raising it when the line goes down.

If these tones do not fit into your way of speaking and you prefer to say the sentence raising or lowering your pitches in different places to those indicated, please be yourself and do it your way.

Now stand confidently and, breathing from the base of your lungs, say the same line as if you are talking to a large hall of people. Be aware of your breathing, articulation, tones, emphasis and volume. Do this 10 times; how do you feel? I hope you feel more confident about speaking to a group of people.

To Find Any Voice Weakness
After practising these relaxation and voice exercises for a few days, ask a friend or relative to listen to you from the other side of a room while you give them information about your course or meeting. Ask them to give you their unbiased opinion of the way you spoke by answering the following questions: Did you come across as relaxed and confident? Did they find your voice pleasant? Could they hear every word? Did your voice tones have variety with correct emphasis? Was your pace of speech right? Did you convey your enthusiasm for your subject?

If they could not answer any of the questions satisfactorily, continue practising the relevant exercises. Also, practise all the exercises for a few days before you run your courses or meetings.

CHAPTER TWO

YOUR TEACHING ENVIRONMENT

By the end of Chapter Two you will:

- Have an idea of the advantages and disadvantages of different types of venue

- Know how to prepare a room for a spiritual meeting

- Realise the importance of ensuring your students are relaxed and that you know various relaxation methods

The Venue

When you decide to run a spiritual meeting or course you will need to have an appropriate venue or room. It should be a place where you will not have interruptions or noise from other people, telephones, traffic or any other disruptions. It should have a relaxed, inviting, warm atmosphere with positive energies and soft colours. When choosing a venue consider the following:

- Is it a suitable size for the numbers you expect?

- Are the energies in the room appropriate for your spiritual meeting?

- Is the room decorated in the right manner for your gathering?

- Is it warm or are you able to control the heating? A room should not be too hot, because people will tend to fall asleep, but if a room is too cold your participants will be uncomfortable, which will reduce their learning ability.

- Is there access to natural light? Being in artificial light all day can affect people's energy levels and mood.

- Are there toilet facilities nearby?

- What drink and/or food facilities are there?

- Do the owners mind you lighting candles?

- Is it accessible by public transport?

- Is there adequate car parking?

- Are there disabled toilets and access?

- If it is not ideal, can you enhance it?

Types of Venue

Many people run spiritual meetings from their own home. You will obviously need a fairly large room with enough chairs for all your attendees and one for yourself. The advantages of running a meeting from your home are that it is cheap, as you will not have to hire a venue, and you will not lose money in rent if you do not have the numbers you hope for. Also, you can have the room just as you want it. The disadvantages are that you will only be able to accommodate a small number of people, depending on the size of your room. Also, unless you are able to dedicate a room in your home to a meeting room, you will probably have to move furniture around in an existing room, usually the lounge. It may disrupt family life, as your family may not be able to make any noise or use the bathroom while your meeting is running. You may feel that you will need extra home contents insurance cover, but you could ask the beings that you resonate with to help you with this. You may also have restrictions from your landlord or there may be constraints in the deeds of your property concerning running a business from home.

In the UK, you will not usually need planning permission to run your business from home as long as it does not take up over half of your house and it does not change the overall character of your dwelling. However, do check with your local authority.

Also, in the UK, you will not have to pay business rates if your room is a multi-purpose room, e.g. you use your lounge as a meeting room or the meeting room has a sofa bed for guests to stay. However, this does vary between local authorities, so check with yours.

You could convert an existing building or build a purpose-built area, such as a summer house, for your meetings if you have a large garage or garden. The advantages of this are the same as using a room in your house, plus it will not disrupt family life, especially if there is a separate entrance. The disadvantages are that you will have large costs, because of the building work, which may be in the form of a loan or remortgaging. Therefore, you have to be confident that you will be able to cover the outlay, and you may need extra building and contents insurance. Also, check the deeds of your property about running a business from home and contact your local council about planning permission, building regulations and business rates.

Renting a venue for your gathering is your best option if you anticipate running meetings and courses for a larger number of people or you do not want to use or do not have the facilities at your home. Look for a suitable venue at village or town halls, upstairs or in back rooms of new age shops, hotels, conference centres or dedicated spiritual centres. Rooms are usually hired at a daily or hourly rate, and some provide refreshments at a cost.

The advantages of hiring a room are that, being in the community, it will give you a greater sense of professionalism, the room will usually have seating and toilet facilities and some will also have kitchens, flip charts, projectors, tables etc. The disadvantages are that you may not be able to hire the room when you would like and the room may not be to your liking. You will also have to travel to your venue and take all the items that you need for your gathering with you. You will have to pay the hire charge even if you have only a few people to your meetings, and so you may not be able to cover the cost of the room.

Cleansing the Area

When you start to prepare your room, and just before your meeting, you must cleanse your room from any negative and unwanted energies that have been left there from the previous users or beings. This may be recently or energy that may have become stuck in the fabric of the building from many months or even many years ago.

To cleanse a room you need to have the intention of sending the unwanted lower-vibrational energies away. To prevent them affecting anybody or anything else, ask the beings that you resonate with to help raise the energies of the unwanted vibrations so that they do no harm to any person, being, animal, entity or thing. When you have cleared the area, again connect with your higher beings, but, this time, ask them to replace the unwanted energies in the room with positive energy appropriate for your venue, you and your students.

There are various methods of room and house cleansing, but all involve walking around the area employing a cleansing method. You will need to pay special attention to corners where stale energies collect. You can use just one technique or combine two or three methods. These purifying techniques can be used to clear unwanted energies from any building. Some different ways of room cleansing are:

- Clapping your hands around the room and other relevant areas. Energy can be moved with sharp sounds coupled with intention. This is the easiest way to clear a room, as it does not involve having or purchasing any other objects and is just as effective as any other method.

- Chiming Tibetan cymbals or striking singing bowls are a way to produce sharp sounds which are pleasing to the ear. If you are using singing bowls, you need to strike them with the gong to produce a sharp noise rather than rolling the gong around the outside of the bowl in the usual singing way.

- Sprinkling blessed water around your area. Use a bowl of water, preferably rain or filtered, and ask the beings that you resonate with to bless it and have the intention that, by their blessing, the energy of the water will be raised. Then dip your fingers into the bowl and flick the water in different directions to cleanse the space where it lands.

- Wafting the smoke from joss, incense or sage smudge sticks can have a pleasant aroma, but be aware that these can cause breathing problems for people who suffer from asthma and other respiratory conditions. Also, use chemical-free sticks, because artificial chemicals contain cancer-causing compounds and are not environmentally friendly.

- Signing appropriate symbols around the room, e.g. reiki symbols, is also a good method if you have been trained in the appropriate discipline.

You should also use these cleansing methods in the kitchen, toilets and the whole area where your students are likely to go.

Room Preparation

You can prepare for your meeting on the day or the day before. Look around your room when you first enter it and clear out any clutter. Think about where you want to put things and imagine how you want it to look and feel. Dirt or dust can hold unwanted energies, so you may need to physically clean it too.

When you prepare your room for your meeting think about how you would like the seating to be arranged. Most spiritual gatherings have chairs around the room in a circle, so that no one person is any more or less important than anybody else, including the tutor. However, you may like to have your chairs in rows, but make sure that people at the back will be able to see and hear you.

To create the right atmosphere for a spiritual meeting you may like to burn candles, as long as the owners of the venue do not object. Most candles are made from paraffin oil, but burning mineral oil candles is not environmentally friendly, because they pollute the atmosphere and may cause lung cancer if used regularly every day. Alternative candles are beeswax or pure vegetable oil candles, such as soya wax. Natural wax and vegetable oil candles create a wonderful atmosphere in the room and they do not smell like paraffin oil candles when extinguished. If you cannot use candles and need lighting, use soft lights such as table lights around the room to create the ambience.

It is lovely to have light relaxing music playing softly in the background, especially when people arrive. For this you will need to have a CD player and a number of different CDs with appropriate music that is at the right tempo. It is best to choose music that does not have any singing, as the words may interfere with what you are saying. Be aware that people who are hard of hearing may find the music distracting, as your voice may merge with the music, making it difficult for them to hear your words.

You may also like to decorate your room with appropriate pictures for your meeting, e.g. angel pictures for an angel gathering. Plants make the room come alive, but be careful with scented flowers as these can aggravate hay fever sufferers, even in the winter. You may also like to put some of your personal spiritual ornaments around the space to help to make it a beautiful, high-vibrational, relaxing place to be.

When you have finished setting up your room, go out and then come back in and, as you do, look around your room as if you are entering for the first time. Does it feel welcoming? Is it relaxing? What are the energies like? What catches your eye?

Making People Feel Welcome

Relaxation

When people come to your meetings you need to ensure that you produce the right environment for learning, and for this students need to be relaxed and comfortable. People coming to a gathering for the first time will probably feel anxious, especially if they come on their own and are meeting others for the first time. Some may have had a difficult journey getting to your venue, others may have had to overcome ridicule at home about coming to a spiritual meeting by relatives who are not yet on their spiritual path or there may be other tensions. When your students arrive, try to make sure that you are there to greet them personally, and, as you do so, smile. A smile is a brilliant way to break the tension and help them feel that the anxiety of coming to your meeting was worth it.

Talking is usually the best way to help people relax, so you should try to get people conversing as soon as they arrive. Providing a hot drink can also aid relaxation and help to prompt conversation. However, if this does not work, you might like to have a set of spiritual cards handy and, while you are waiting for everyone to arrive, you can ask each of the participants who are present to pick a card and then talk about why they feel they have drawn that card that day.

Sometimes somebody who has said they would come does not turn up. This can have an impact on a small group, because there will obviously be a vacant chair and everyone will know somebody has not come, so remove the chair as soon as it is obvious that they are not going to arrive. Do not wait for latecomers to arrive for more than five minutes before you start, because

30

people who came on time will be paying for the full meeting and should not be penalised.

If somebody arrives late, make sure that they are welcomed into the group and then briefly recap, as quickly as you can, on what you have covered so far. There is usually a genuine reason for somebody being late, because most people do not like to interrupt a meeting that has already started, so treat them kindly, even though it is an annoying disruption to your gathering and time table.

Another way to help people relax is to know the names of others in the group. You can use name tags, which is good to help you and others remember names if you have a large meeting, but it does tend to make people lazy at memorising. Also, people may put their name tags on an outer garment and if they get hot they may take the garment off and the name tag will no longer be visible. Also, the name tag may become obscured by long hair. The choice of whether to use name tags is up to you, but it is not usually necessary to use them with small groups.

Ice-breakers

Ice-breakers are designed to help people talk, learn names and discover a bit about others in the group. However, some ice-breakers can be a bit intimidating for shy people. When using ice-breakers, it is good if you, the leader, do your bit to break the ice first, so that people get an idea of what is required from them. There are many different ice-breakers, and the type of ice-breaker you use depends on the number of students and the time you have available. Some ice-breakers that you may like to try:

- Ask everyone in turn to say their name, and also choose what else you want people to talk about from the following:
  o Where they live.
  o A bit about themselves.
  o A bit about their spiritual journey.
  o Why they have come to the meeting.

  This is the most common ice-breaker, and is fine for people who are not too anxious or shy, but many people miss what those who went before them say because they are too busy trying to think of what they are going to say when it is their turn. This ice-breaker is good for smaller groups where there is a fair amount of time available.

- Have a ball, teddy bear or some other object for the participants to throw to somebody who then says their bit. When they have done this they then throw it to someone who has not yet had a turn. This way people do not know when they will be required to speak and it can be a bit of fun, as tension will be reduced if somebody does not catch the object or it goes off course etc. You can ask people to just say their name when the object is thrown to them or any of the points in the previous ice-breaker depending on the amount of time you have.

- Have some pre-prepared pairs of objects, e.g. pairs of the same picture, flowers, leaves or some other articles. Ask your participants to pick one object each and then find the person who has the same object as them. Ask them to talk in turns with that partner about any of the items listed in the first ice-breaker according to the time that you have. This ice-breaker is good for shy people, because they get to talk on a one-to-one basis. However, people only get to know the one person and not the whole group.

- Each participant in turn says their name and something that they like. For example, "My name is .... and I like gardening." Here people have something to associate with each person. This ice-breaker is quick and not as intimidating for shy people, so it is ideal if you have a large group with only a few minutes scheduled for an ice-breaker.

- Have a pack of spiritual cards that have a picture and some writing on them. It helps if you have cards that reflect the subject matter of your gathering. For example, have some angel cards for an angel meeting. Then, if you have not done this while waiting for others to arrive, ask everybody to pick a card in turn and say their name as well as what is written on the card. If you have time you can expand it to ask them why they feel they have chosen that particular card. This ice-breaker takes the focus off the individual and onto the card, so it is less daunting.

- Each participant, in turn, says their name with a positive adjective in front of it and the other members of the group greet the person. The adjective can be something they aspire to be or something they feel comfortable and happy with. It often flows better if the adjective begins with the same letter as the name, but some people find this difficult to achieve. For example, a participant called Bert says, "Hello, I am brilliant Bert." The rest of the group reply together, "Hello, brilliant Bert."

This ice-breaker helps the group to integrate, as they are replying together as one and it is fairly quick, although you will need to give them time to think of a positive adjective before you start.

- If you are running a course over more than a day, you may have time to ask your participants to pair with one another and then ask them to take it in turns to smile, greet and compliment the other person, e.g. something they are wearing or their happy smile. Then tell the other person a bit about themselves on a one-to-one basis. When they have finished talking and listening with one person they move on to another member of the group, and so on, until they have spoken on a one-to-one basis with everybody. This is more comfortable for shy people, but it can take a long time, depending on the number of people in your meeting. You must be strict with timing and inform the group from the beginning that they have a set amount of time, e.g. five minutes, to speak and listen to each person. You will need to clap your hands, chime some Tibetan cymbals or have some other way of making a noise that can be heard over a group of talking people to indicate that it is time to change partners.

Feeling Safe

During most spiritual meetings and courses it is usual for some, if not all, members to have the opportunity to share personal information, some of which may be confidential. This can be intimidating for some people when they are in a room full of strangers. It is important to make your students feel safe so that they can relax, be themselves, share and learn from this experience. Therefore, you need to ask everyone at the beginning of the meeting to agree that personal matters, which may arise during the gathering, will be treated in confidence. You need to ask every member of the group to give their nod of agreement or raise their hand to agree that personal matters discussed during the meeting will stay within the confines of the group and will not be shared with any other person. However, make people aware that they do not have to disclose personal information if they do not want to and they are in control of their own personal boundaries. It can help your students to relax and build trust in you if you share some of your life experiences with them, even some things that did not go quite right, as we are all human and have our own challenges.

During your gathering, be open and allow members of the group to have their say and ask questions. You may like to tell your students at the beginning of your meeting that they can ask questions as you go or that there will be time allotted at the end for questions, depending on how you prefer to run your meetings. This will help your students to relax further knowing that they can ask for clarification if they do not understand something.

During spiritual meetings people often receive revealing information or issues (past or present) may surface which can make them go into emotional shock. This is because it is too much for them to process at once. Symptoms of this are crying; holding their breath; feeling cold or clammy; becoming ungrounded; not being able to focus clearly; or, if badly shocked, not being able to move freely. The person may or may not realise what is happening; however, either way, they will need your support and that of the other members of the group.

If, or when, you have a participant in emotional shock, you will need to briefly tell the others in the group what is happening and ask for their help and support for the person. Help to support them as follows:

- If they are crying, let them cry as much as is needed, because crying releases emotions. Supply tissues and let other members of the group empathise with them.

- If they are holding their breath, which is a defence against sensing feelings, they will not realise that they are doing so. You and the other group members should remind them to breathe regularly until they are breathing normally.

- If they are feeling cold and clammy, make sure they are seated or lying down and cover them with a blanket.

- If they are ungrounded, take steps to ground them. Grounding is covered in Chapter Three: *Good Spiritual Teaching Practice*.

- If they are not focusing correctly or cannot move freely, reassure them by explaining what is happening and tell them that the experience will soon pass.

- Lead the group to ask the beings that you resonate with or are studying in your meeting to help the person process their issues.

When they are feeling better, allow them to talk about the issue while you and your other group members listen, empathise and, if appropriate, give useful, tactful suggestions. If you are running a healing course, you may like to offer them some group healing. This will obviously take you away from your course material, but I believe everything happens for a reason, so go with whatever happens. On the positive side, as all members of the group have had a part in the events, it helps to bring them together and they may have learned something from it. If these occasions worry you, I have found that we are never given anything that we cannot handle, even though we may be challenged at times.

Information at the Beginning of Meetings

It helps course participants to relax more if they know what to expect during the time they are with you and where to find necessary things. Therefore, you need to tell them where the toilets are and what arrangements have been made for food and drinks. It helps people if they know roughly when any breaks and lunch (if it is a day course) are going to be and how long. It is also helpful to confirm the finishing time. If you have spiritual cards, books or items for sale let them know if they can look at them and handle the cards during breaks and lunch times. If you are renting a venue, the owners will probably want you to explain the fire procedures, which you must do at the beginning of your meeting.

An important point at the start of a gathering, which may have an impact on the enjoyment of the meeting, is to ask all attendees to turn off their mobile phones. Some people happily do this, while others may want to put their mobile phones on silent mode. I always ask people to turn them off, because the electromagnetic energy emissions from the phones are of a different frequency to our natural energies. This has the effect of reducing the size and energy of our auras and, as a result, we are not able to connect as well with the higher realms. This is, obviously, not a good thing in a spiritual meeting.

People will be anxious about what you will be doing during the meeting, so it helps to give a brief summary of your subject matter as well as telling them that you will be running some visualisations, meditations and activities, if appropriate.

Another way to help people relax and talk is to give them some paper and a pen and ask them to write down what they are expecting to get out of the meeting. It helps to have some clipboards for your attendees to rest on while writing. When everyone has finished, ask each one, in turn, to say what they have written. You can then either confirm or deny that you will be covering that subject, or, if they want help with an aspect of their life, you may like to suggest that when you give them the opportunity to connect with the beings of light that you are bringing into the meeting, they ask them for help. However, I have had some people say that they hope to be introduced to their soul mate or perfect partner, and if this, or something similar, happens to you, then politely say that this will be unlikely during the meeting, but they may like to contact the beings of the higher realms for help in this matter. This activity can also be treated as an ice-breaker, as it helps to get people talking. You can also ask people to keep it handy for the end of the course and then talk about it to see if they have achieved their goals.

We have covered a number of things you can do at the beginning of spiritual meetings during this section, so I will briefly recap on all the points for you to choose what you feel is right to use for you and your group:

- Greet each person and smile when they arrive – important.

- Provide hot drinks.

- Use spiritual cards while waiting for others to arrive.

- Provide name tags.

- Have a confidentiality agreement – important.

- Provide an ice-breaker.

- Inform students where the toilet facilities are – important.

- Inform students about food and drink arrangements – important.

- Inform students of fire procedures – essential if the owners of the venue have requested this.

- Ask students to turn off their mobile phones – essential.

- Inform students of the times of breaks, including a lunch break if it is an all-day meeting, how long they will be and the time the meeting will end – important.

- Inform students if they can handle your cards or books during breaks.

- Inform students of any items you may have for sale.

- Give students a brief summary of your intended subject matter – important.

- Inform students when they can ask questions.

- Ask students to write down and talk about what they are expecting to get out of the meeting.

CHAPTER THREE

GOOD SPIRITUAL TEACHING PRACTICE

By the end of Chapter Three you will:

- Know how to present yourself and your work as well as care for your students

- Have an awareness of your group's energy and be able to keep it high

- Have an understanding of what to do about troublesome and disruptive behaviour

- Know about grounding and protecting others

- Be able to safely open and close group sessions

Presentation and Caring for your Group

The way that you present yourself and your work as well as care for your students will have a big impact on them, their enjoyment of the course and, ultimately, their ability to learn. One of the most important factors is your passion for your subject matter. When people sense you teaching from your heart they will be enthused.

You also need to know the material you are teaching extremely well; however, remember that it is impossible to know everything. If you are asked a question that you do not know the answer to, say so. You may like to ask members of your group if they know the answer, and, if they do, it will empower them and make them feel good. Otherwise, you can say that you will find out and get back to them. If you say this, then make sure that you do.

Another strong aspect which has already been mentioned, but is important, is to be yourself. When you stand in your own light, teaching in a confident, caring, honest way, with your own personal, unique style, people will love being taught by you.

Other techniques that help to give a good, professional, enjoyable presentation and meeting:

- When standing or sitting, do so in a confident way. So stand up or sit up straight, without slouching, and do not tilt your head to one side. Also, when standing, do not lean your body weight on one hip. Just standing or sitting in the correct way will make you feel more self-assured.

- Do not fiddle with hair, jewellery, clothes or anything else, because these actions do not indicate confidence.

- When you are unsure about something do not look down or up, because others will subconsciously realise your uncertainty.

- Your group will enjoy the meeting if they are comfortably seated and know about toilet, food and drink facilities and arrangements.

- Make eye contact with every member of your group as this helps people to feel they are special and raises their vibrations, which helps them connect with higher energies. This is easier if people are sitting in a circle.

- Try to treat everybody the same and do not favour or ignore any one individual. You will need to be aware of your personal discriminations and typecasting of people. If you find somebody is being challenging, think if this is a reflection of your own views and attitudes. Also, find the lessons that are to be learned from this situation and give this person help if they need it.

- Try to get everybody involved and encourage them to contribute. This can be difficult if somebody is very talkative and hogs the limelight while others are shy. However, try to ask the shy people questions or their opinion to bring them into the conversation. This will help with their enjoyment of the meeting, as they will feel included.

- See the best in your participants and their work and compliment them on it. People learn by encouragement, not by being criticised. If somebody is struggling, find something to praise about them and build on this, so they feel encouraged to do more. However, do not forget to compliment people who are competent, because they need to feel they are doing well too.

- Before the meeting, do relaxation, breathing, tone, articulation and voice pace exercises as explained in the *Preparing your Voice* section in Chapter One. These will help you to speak confidently and keep your voice strong with the right inflections at the end of your sentences.

- When talking, get to the point quickly, otherwise the information you give out will become boring and you will lose your group's attention. Also, do not use filler words or phrases such as "um", "awfully", "know what I mean" or saying "sorry" when it is not necessary, as these can also lead to boredom for your participants and can symbolise a lack of self-confidence.

- Do not ignore difficult behaviour. This must be dealt with as soon as you can, because it will ruin the meeting for others as well as you. Details of dealing with difficult behaviour can be found later in this section.

- When delivering the meeting, keep to the subject matter. Participants will have come to learn about what you have advertised and may not be prepared or not want to know about something else, and so could become bored or frustrated. If a participant starts to talk about something that is not relevant to the meeting, politely interrupt and tell them that although what they are saying is interesting, people are there to hear about your advertised subject and they can discuss their topic with others at break or lunch time. Other participants will usually be happy with this.

- Make sure that you keep to the times you have advertised or stated, because people may have to telephone somebody in a break or lunch time, they may have arranged to be being picked up from the meeting or they may have to catch public transport. If you find that the meeting is going to overrun, tell your participants and give them the opportunity to leave on time if they need to.

- To help make points come alive or something spiritual become relevant in day-to-day situations, narrate stories, which can be personal or accounts from others. However, do not rely heavily on your own tales, because too many may be perceived as boasting. If you are using a story about or from another person, keep the person's identity anonymous, unless they are happy for you to discuss the story in your meetings.

- To help you have a really great meeting, practise positive affirmations or statements about it and your participants, as described in Chapter One in *Personal Preparation for Teaching* on page 13. Another example of an affirmation you can use before a meeting is, "My meeting is a great success and there are many positive participants who are benefiting from it in a huge way."

Working With your Group's Energy

When running your meeting, keep an eye on your group's energy levels. This can be checked by looking at their body language and, if you are sensitive, being perceptive of their energy vibrations. If people's energy levels start to drop, you need to find a way to raise them as soon as you can. This means that you need to be fluid in your presentation and able to change your meeting plan slightly.

Body language is usually a subconscious expression of inner moods and emotions. Common forms of discontented body language that you may come across in meeting situations are having a bored or unhappy facial expression, sitting with folded arms, yawning, resting the chin in a hand or fiddling with clothes/something else. If you have a number of people with unhappy energy, you need to change your strategy and raise their vibrations. There is no point continuing with your presentation if people are not taking it in.

The main way to keep the energy high in a meeting is to have a good mix of:

- Information.

45

- Meditations or visualisations.
- Activities.

This can be achieved, for example, by giving them some information, then a meditation on the information and, finally, doing an activity about it. This could be telling them about a higher being, then visualise to meet a higher being and, afterwards, draw a picture of the being or what was seen in the visualisation. We will talk about visualisation and meditation in Chapter Four and activities in Chapter Five.

If the energy levels of your meeting are still going down, a good way to raise them is to get your participants talking. You may like to ask them to share their experiences and ideas or ask them if they have any questions on something you have just presented. Activities such as dancing, lively music, drama, drawing and laughter raise energies. Another way to raise the energy of your group is to have a short impromptu break, where participants can walk around and get some fresh air. This could be combined with an activity, e.g. looking at the auras of the plants outside.

Pay attention to the environment of the room. If it is stuffy open a window, or if the temperature is not right then adjust it. If people have just eaten, their energy will be being used to digest their food and they will find it difficult to concentrate on what you are saying, so an activity would be more appropriate at this time.

However, some people may appear to have lower energy levels when they may simply be quietly reflecting on your previous statement; you need to work with your intuition.

You may get the feeling that your group's energy is low because they did not understand something you just explained. If this is the case, you can ask them if they would like you to go over the point again to clear up any confusion. When you explain it again, make sure that you explain it in a different way, because if they did not understand the first time they heard it they will not understand the same words the second time either.

If you find just one person with negative energy, it may be something to do with this person and not your delivery. If they are an outgoing type, you may like to ask them directly if they are feeling all right or if they do not understand something. However, if you feel that being singled out might embarrass them, wait until you have a break and then have a quiet word with them to find out what the problem is.

Listening to Members of your Group
An important aspect of teaching is to listen and actually hear and feel what your group members are telling you. Have you overheard, or even participated in, a conversation where somebody may not have heard the other person correctly and replies, but they are talking about a totally different topic? It is a wonderful heartfelt gift to listen with complete attention and without judgement to what another person is saying. This can be achieved relatively easily with somebody that you like and admire, but can be testing with somebody that you do not resonate with.

Most of us hear what is being said to us, but we are often so busy trying to formulate a reply that we miss the underlying message and the way the other person is actually feeling. We also tend to interpret other people's words in our own way.

You may like to practise your listening skills by taking it in turns to totally pay attention to a short story that a friend or relative is saying by using the following pointers:

- Give the other person your total attention.

- Try to understand their feelings and emotions and, if appropriate, mirror their body language to help give you an idea of their sentiments.

- Avoid formulating a reply.

- Let them finish without any interruptions.

- When they have finished, do not think that you have to say something immediately. It is fine to reflect on what they have said for a number of seconds.

- Thank them for their story and then repeat it back to them to check that you have heard and understood it correctly and assessed their emotions accurately.

- Allow the other person to have their own opinions and beliefs, but you can inform them of yours so that you both have a bigger understanding.

- If they have a problem, do not feel that you need to have an answer to their situation. Often, having somebody to really listen to them lifts a big weight off their shoulders.

Troublesome Behaviour
Troublesome behaviour can take many different forms, and usually the person displaying these actions is not aware of their influence on others. This kind of behaviour is annoying and can reduce the enjoyment of the meeting for others, and so must be stopped.

One common form of troublesome behaviour in group meetings is people talking to others while you are presenting your information. To deal with this, stop talking and look at the person until they realise that everybody is listening to their conversation. They usually stop, apologise and do not do it again.

There is often a domineering person within a group who likes to talk loudly and at length. To deal with this person, raise your forearm from the elbow in a stopping gesture, thank them for their input and then sweep your gaze away. This is a very powerful signal and should not be overused. If their behaviour is still a nuisance, when you come back from a break, say that you will be changing chairs. When you see where this person is sitting, sit beside them. This way they do not catch your eye and cannot dominate so much.

Sometimes there is an 'expert' in the group who tends to know 'everything'. This can be very challenging for you and you must handle the situation calmly and with care. If the expert makes a valid contribution, then acknowledge their input and knowledge. If you do not resonate with their views, say so, but in a composed way without attacking their beliefs. Also, do not allow the expert to dominate. It is your meeting and you need to teach what you have prepared.

If you are running a meeting over a day or a number of days, you may find that there is a student who consistently arrives back late from breaks. If you wait for them to arrive, other group members will not appreciate always having to wait for one person, and it can have an accumulative effect on your scheduled plan. If this is happens, make sure that you always start on time and do not recap for the consistently late person.

Disruptive Behaviour

Occasionally, one person's behaviour disrupts you, your presentation and your other group members. It is your job to keep this disturbance to a minimum, because it will affect the enjoyment as well as the learning ability for other group members.

Disruptive behaviour can generate emotional responses in people. You cannot help the emotions of other members of your group; but, because they will look to you for leadership in this situation, you must lead by example and deal with the circumstances in a professional, calm and effective manner.

To deal with this disruptive person you must:

- Make them aware of what is happening by explaining the events in a calm, composed way without attacking or blaming them. For example, "During the previous session, you shouted at me because you disagreed with my views."

- Express how you feel with a calm, unemotional approach without compromising their feelings. For example, "I was upset that you shouted at me and I could see that others were also disturbed."

- Tell them, very clearly and without confrontation, what you want from them. For example, "It is good that you have different beliefs from me and are able to say so. However, I would like you to express your views calmly, without shouting or insulting me or other members of the group."

The above approach usually defuses the situation, but, very occasionally, the person may continue with their bad behaviour. If this happens, you have to take a stand and tell them what you will do if they do not change. For example, "I have asked you to express your opinions without shouting or insulting me or other members of the group. If you can convey your beliefs in a calm way, we will be able to understand your viewpoint, but if you continue to shout and insult us, then I will have no option but to ask you to leave." If they still continue, then you must carry out your stipulation. This person will not be happy about leaving; however, for your sake and the sake of the other participants, you must remain composed and stand your ground.

When reflecting on the meeting afterwards, if you have had a disruptive person in your group, you should contemplate if any of your own views or actions were being reflected back to you. If so, you must work on yourself to make sure something similar does not happen again. There are usually lessons to be learned from the situation on both sides, and also consider the possibility that the other person may need help or their actions may have been a plea for assistance.

Grounding and Protection

A very important aspect of spiritual teaching is to make sure all the members of your group are grounded, as well as safe from unwanted energies. I have heard stories of people walking around in a daze after attending a spiritual gathering because they were not grounded properly or had picked up an unwanted energy.

Grounding

When we connect with higher beings and energies our vibrations naturally rise, but because we are incarnated into a physical world we need to be connected with our planet earth. We are grounded when our soul is fully in our physical body and connected to the earth. When we sleep, meditate, have healing or do other spiritual work our soul usually moves out of our body and returns to the spiritual planes. Normally, our soul completely returns to our body, but sometimes it does not fully come back and gets stuck, partially in and partially out. This is when we are said to be 'ungrounded'.

Being ungrounded can be very uncomfortable, disorientating and, in some cases, dangerous. At the physical level, signs of being ungrounded are feeling sick; feeling dizzy; feeling spaced out; feeling faint; getting a headache; or, occasionally, feeling panicky. Some people have a tendency to become ungrounded more easily than others. Therefore, it is essential that you ground participants both before and after your group sessions, as well as before and after visualising and meditating. Also, be vigilant during the meeting for anybody showing signs of being ungrounded. If you suspect that their soul is not fully in their body, ground them before you continue, because they will not be able to absorb anything else until this is done.

To follow, there are a number of ways to ground people. Different grounding methods are more effective for some than others, so, if you are grounding an individual, if one method does not work, try another one.

- Visualise big, thick roots growing down from the bottom of the ungrounded person's feet. Push these roots deep into the ground. Ask the person to feel the earth's energies through their roots and connect with her. This is especially good for use before, during and after visualisations, meditations and healing.

- With the ungrounded person sitting on a chair, stand behind them and place your hands on their shoulders for about 30 seconds, with the intention of grounding. Next, very firmly, stroke down the sides of the top of their arms, while you ask the other members of the group to visualise the ungrounded person's roots growing down from their feet and deep into the earth; the more energy that goes into it the more powerful it will be. Continue for a few minutes. If one individual is ungrounded, working collectively brings the group together and helps to prevent boredom.

- Kneel on the floor and place your hands firmly, but calmly, on the top of the ungrounded person's feet for a few minutes, while focusing on grounding them. At the same time, visualise roots growing from the person's feet into the earth. Also, ask the person you are grounding and other members of the group to visualise their roots growing down into the earth and connecting with our planet. This, again, can bring the group together and stop others from becoming bored.

- Stamping feet, clapping hands, stretching, dancing and walking can all have a grounding effect, and everybody can join in. These actions can also be used to raise energy levels, and they are even more beneficial if they are done outside, especially if carried out barefoot on the grass!

- Actively consuming food and drink, especially carbohydrates or a hot non-caffeinated drink, can ground some people. If it is convenient, you may like to have an early break, and make sure the ungrounded person has a hot drink and a biscuit.

- Being outside and breathing fresh air into the lungs and blood-stream can be beneficial.

- Holding the wrists, especially the palm side, under cold running water for three or four minutes is effective for some, since many nerve endings and reflexes pass through the wrists.

Protection

We need protection because, when we raise our energy vibrations through visualisation, meditation and/or connecting with the higher energies, our energy receptors (chakras) open much wider and our auras expand. This makes us open to all energies, including lower vibrations.

I am sure that you know that as well as high-vibrational energies there are also lower-vibrational, or negative, energies. Most negative energies come from other people, buildings or beings from other realms. If our energy receptors are wide open and we are not protected, these energies can enter our energy systems and have the power to lower our vibrations and adversely affect us physically, emotionally and mentally. This can make us uncomfortable and ill. It is essential to make sure that you and your participants are safe from unwanted energies by protecting individuals, the group as a whole, the room and the building, if appropriate. However, it is best not to talk to your group about lower energies, because what people think about can actually happen. As the purpose of spiritual meetings is to raise vibrations to connect with higher energies, talking about negative entities will have a counter effect.

When running a meeting it is essential to protect everyone at the beginning, when visualising or meditating and at the close of the meeting, as well as any other time you feel it is necessary. If anybody leaves the environment, e.g. going out at lunchtime, then protection should also be done at the close of the morning session and at the opening of the afternoon session.

A protection that somebody believes in, will work for them, and you will find that people resonate better with some methods than others. Therefore, you need to do at least two methods each time, so if somebody does not resonate with the first method then they should be able to do so with the second. Protection is usually done as a form of visualisation. The techniques of visualisation are explained in Chapter Four.

There are innumerable methods of protection, below are some examples.
Protection for individuals:
  • Visualise being inside a sphere of reflective white light tinged with pink, the colour of love, with the reflective side facing outwards, so that anything that is not of a higher vibration is reflected away from you with love.

- Visualise being within a bubble of high-vibrational white, or another meaningful colour, pure light. Know that only that which is of the highest and purest vibration may enter the bubble, so you are totally safe and protected.

- Ask the higher beings for protection. For example, say, "Guides of protection, please can you surround me, protect me and keep me safe, thank you."

- Visualise standing in the centre of a large pink rose. Let the rose close its petals around you. Feel or sense the protection and the love that the rose is giving you.

- Invite your guardian angel, or another angel, to surround you with their wings, so keeping you safe and enfolded with their wonderful high-vibrational, loving energy.

- Visualise a higher being or a meaningful symbol, such as a reiki symbol, in front of you, another one behind you, one to your right, one to your left, one above you and one below you. Ask the beings or symbols to keep you safe and free from harm.

- Call on Archangel Michael to place his deep-blue cloak of protection around you. Sense him placing it lovingly over your shoulders, pulling it gently under your feet, slowly zipping up the front and tenderly pulling the hood over your head, so that you feel protected, snug and safe within it.

Protection for the group:
- Use a protection affirmation by asking your participants to say it three times, after you lead, one sentence at a time. For example, "We, as a group, are surrounded by a pure bubble of white/golden/crystal light. Only that which is of the highest and purest vibration may enter this space. We are totally safe and protected."

- Invite the higher beings that you are working with to come into the room and form a circle surrounding your group. Ask your participants to sense them and know that they are offering safety and protection.

- Any of the first four examples as listed in *Protection for individuals*.

Protection for the building or room:
- Visualise a quartz or crystal pyramid being placed over the building or room. Then visualise an inverted pyramid coming up from the centre of the earth and joining the first one at ground level, so forming a shape (an octahedron) with the building or room in the centre. Know that the whole building or room is totally safe and protected within the octahedron.

- Any of the examples listed in *Protection for the group*.

These are just some examples of protection. Please use what you feel will resonate for your participants and the topic of your meeting.

Safely Opening and Closing Group Sessions

When running a spiritual meeting, your participants must be grounded and protected at the beginning of a session as well as at the end. It can also help to raise their energies at the beginning and to make sure they leave in a safe condition at the end of the session. This is usually done with a short visualisation, and is called 'opening' at the beginning of a session and 'closing' at the end of a session. Visualisation techniques will be discussed in Chapter Four.

Opening
The reason that we open at the beginning of a session is:

- To help people relax and settle.
- To bring the awareness of the participants to the spiritual work ahead.
- To ground everybody present before starting, in case they arrived ungrounded.
- For protection, which makes sure only higher energies can come in during the session.
- To help raise the vibrations of the participants, so that they can easily connect with higher energies and beings.

Participants' energies can be raised by simply connecting with higher vibrations. This can be done by asking them to surround themselves with a coloured bubble/column of light appropriate for the energies you will be working with or asking the higher beings to come forward and let themselves be known.

To open a session, remember the following acronym:

GPR – Great Physical Realms

> **G** = Grounding
>
> **P** = Protecting
>
> **R** = Raising energies

Many spiritual people spend so much time trying to experience the spiritual planes of existence that they sometimes lose appreciation for the physical realms. When in the physical realms we can experience touch and taste, but those in the spiritual planes cannot do this. We have a beautiful physical world full of plants and creatures to take care of and appreciate. Whether you resonate with what I am saying or not, I hope this will help you to remember GPR.

An example of a typical opening:

- Ground yourself by taking your attention to the bottom of your feet and visualise roots growing into the earth. Let your roots branch out, go deeper and explore inside our planet. Let her molten rock wrap around them, doing them no harm, just loving and nurturing them. Connect with our earth, feel her energies and ground yourself with her. (Grounding).

- Ask your guardian angel to stand behind you and enfold you in their wings. Feel the love, safety and protection your angel is giving you. (The first form of protection).

- Visualise a bubble of pure, shimmering, crystal light surrounding your room. Know that only the highest and purest vibrations can enter the bubble of light. You are totally safe and no harm can come to you within this pure, shimmering, crystal light. (The second form of protection).

- Now see a column of pure-white light coming from the higher realms, through the bubble of crystal light, to you. Breathe this light into your physical body and then out into your aura. As you continue to breathe in this way, your physical body and your aura become full of the high-vibrational white light and your aura expands. Sense your vibrations rising. (Raising energies).

Using GPR is essential for opening a spiritual session. However, you may like to embellish it by adding additional items, e.g. you may like to start by relaxing your students. For this you could say something like: "Sit comfortably and close your eyes. Bring your attention to your head and consciously relax all your head muscles, including your eyes and the muscles around your eyes. When you feel that your head is sufficiently relaxed, bring your attention to your neck muscles and consciously relax these." Continue down the body – the shoulders, the arms and hands, the back, the chest, the hips and, lastly, the legs and feet.

Another item you may like to add to your opening is to invite the higher beings or energies that you are going to be working with into your room and ask your participants to sense their energies. You may also like to ask them to help you and your participants have a great meeting full of fun where everybody receives something that they need.

Closing
The reason that we should close at the end of a session is:

- To prepare people to go into another environment which is not usually of such a high vibration as that of your meeting venue.

- To make your participants' energy receptors a safe size, because their auras and chakras will have expanded and opened wide while doing the spiritual work in your meeting, which makes them vulnerable to unwanted energies. It is not advisable for them to leave the safety of your room without closing them to a normal level.

- To make sure your participants are grounded and protected before they leave your meeting.

To close a session we use the following acronym:

PEG

> **P** = Protect
>
> **E** = Energy awareness
>
> **G** = Ground

The protection is usually just done for individuals, because they are leaving the group and your room, and there is no need to protect these.

Energy awareness simply means to pay attention to your participants' personal energies to make sure they are at a safe level for when they enter unprotected surroundings. To do this, ask them to adjust their auras and major chakras to a size that feels right for them for what they are about to do. When doing this for the chakras give your participants time to work on all of their major chakras; you may like to name the chakras slowly, going down the body one-by-one, so that you are working with your participants.

An example of a typical closing:

- Visualise an angel in front of you, another one behind you, one to your right, one to your left, one above you and one below you. Ask the angels to open their wings and enfold you so that you are surrounded by angels and angels' wings, which will keep you safe and protected on your way home and for the rest of the day. (The first form of protection).

- You find yourself standing in the centre of a gigantic pink rose. Let the rose close its petals gently around you. Sense the protection and the love that the rose is giving you. (The second form of protection).

- Bring your attention to your aura, which has expanded during the meeting. Bring it in to a size that feels right for you, bearing in mind that you will soon be leaving the meeting and going into the outside world. (Energies for the aura).

- Now sense your chakras, which have opened wide during the meeting. Close each one, in turn, to a size that feels right for what you will be doing soon. (Energies for chakras).

- Bring your attention to the bottom of your feet and grow big, thick, strong roots down from the bottom of your feet and into the earth. Push them deeper and deeper until they eventually reach the centre of the earth. Connect with Mother Earth, sense her gentle energy and ground yourself with her. (Grounding).

Using PEG (protect, energy awareness and ground) is essential for closing; but, as with the openings, you may like to add more. You can give thanks to the beings and energies that have been working with you during your meeting or you may like to protect each chakra as you close them to the right size.

After the closing, it is a lovely gesture to blow out candles that you may have had burning and dedicate them as you do so. Examples of the dedication are to your group members, the beings or energies you have been working with or something of current concern in worldwide events. To do this, hold the burning candle and say something like, "I dedicate this candle to the higher beings that have worked with us here today." Then invite all your group members to help you blow it out at the same time.

CHAPTER FOUR

HOW TO LEAD A VISUALISATION OR MEDITATION

By the end of Chapter Four you will:

- Understand about visualisation and meditation and the differences between them

- Know how to prepare and deliver a visualisation

- Be able to run a meditation

Visualisation and Meditation

Visualisation and meditation are the cornerstones of spiritual meetings, as they enhance the information we give our participants, making it personal and applicable for them. People form their connections with the higher realms during visualisations and meditations and receive their individual images and information.

Many think they are meditating when they are actually visualising, but there is a distinct difference. Visualisation involves imagining we are somewhere else and creating the visions, sounds, feelings and aromas in our mind or being led with somebody's voice, either in person or on CD or tape, to form the scene. Examples are a descriptive journey, daydreaming or a manifestation exercise in which we visualise a specific positive outcome.

When we visualise, we have our physical eyes closed and view images on a kind of screen on the inside of our forehead (our third eye chakra). Some people see pictures and others see colours, which, with practice, give way to pictures.

However, some people may not 'see' anything at all, but imagine, sense or just have an inner knowing of what is happening. All these methods are perfectly normal, as each person is a different and unique being.

Meditation, on the other hand, involves the mind being in silence or focusing on a specific object, sound, symbol or thought. In this state, higher energy or beings can easily plant information into our minds, which we may or may not be consciously aware of at the time. Examples are concentrating on an object in front of us, such as a candle, or focusing on a situation, event, problem, some good music or other pleasant sound. A challenging, but rewarding, form of meditation can be completely emptying the mind and allowing it to be totally still.

Regular visualisation and meditation provides many extraordinary benefits, as it helps us to still our minds so we are able to connect easily with the higher realms. It is when our minds are still that we are receptive to new ideas, perspectives, answers, concepts and visions being placed in our consciousness by higher beings. Sometimes we are not aware of this, as we frequently get the insight, guidance or inspiration later.

Regularly stilling the mind affects the physical body by lowering blood pressure, cholesterol and stress hormone levels. People usually feel refreshed after a visualisation or meditation, as it is almost like having a good sleep. Try to encourage your participants to visualise or meditate at home for at least five minutes every day, as this will give them more energy and increase their endorphin levels, which will make them happier, more content, healthier and more relaxed.

Calming the mind takes discipline, practice, patience and focused intention, as well as kindness to ourselves. People often find that they have a day when they find it difficult to still their mind, so tell them that if this happens they need to stop and do something else, not worry about it, and try again the next day. If they try to force it to happen, it will have a detrimental effect.

If you are running a meeting for a group of spiritual beginners, there will probably be some people in the group who have not visualised or meditated before and may feel a bit intimidated at the thought of doing so, especially in front of other people. If this is the case, you can put them at ease by telling them that they are bound to have concentrated on a problem, situation or daydreamed in the past and these are forms of visualisation or meditation, so they have done it before.

When running a visualisation or meditation, you need to make sure your participants are comfortable and sitting at ease, with their backs straight, so that their chakras in the centre of the spine are in a straight line. This makes the connection between heaven and earth stronger and helps with grounding. They must also have their arms and legs uncrossed, because this allows free movement of energy around the body. Additionally, you should ask them to remove their shoes for a better connection to the earth when grounding and take off their watches. Higher beings do not seem to like timepieces, maybe because there is no time, as such, in the spiritual planes.

People connect better with the higher realms when they are relaxed, so always start a visualisation or meditation with some form of relaxation as well as grounding, protecting and raising energies (GPR), unless you have done this very recently. This need not be as detailed for a visualisation or meditation, because you should already have done a comprehensive opening at the beginning of the session.

At the end of the visualisation or meditation you should always ground again and, if you feel it is necessary, protect as well. You also need to keep checking your participants during the session to make sure they are in a safe place. This can be done visually, but it is often better to work with your intuition. If you notice somebody is uncomfortable or distressed, cut the visualisation or meditation short, bring everyone back safely and then check on this person.

You also need to encourage your group to drink plenty of water, because connecting with the higher realms can have a detoxifying effect and the body needs water to flush the toxins away. Many people find that they have a dry mouth when they attend spiritual meetings; this is because their body is telling them that it needs more water.

Preparing and Leading Visualisations

When leading a guided visualisation you are putting ideas and thoughts into your participants' minds, which can have a deep impact on them. Most people follow what is being said, but be aware that occasionally a persons' mind may go somewhere different or they may fall asleep. This is fine, as they usually receive what they need at the time.

There are two ways of leading a guided visualisation:

- Conscious visualisation – where you decide what you want to achieve with the visualisation and plan it accordingly.

- Channelled visualisation – where you do not know where you will be going or what you are going to say in advance as your higher beings guide you to take your group on a journey. This type of visualisation usually comes with experience.

If you are new to leading visualisations, it is better to use a conscious visualisation to begin with, and, as you gain confidence, you may like to try a channelled visualisation.

When conducting a visualisation, the person has their eyes shut and is guided by your voice. Therefore, you need to make sure that the sound of your voice is calming, relaxing and makes people feel safe. You need to practise your voice tones, because raising them helps people connect with the higher realms and lowering them can bring deep relaxation. Practise the exercises in the *Preparing your Voice* section in Chapter One, especially the exercises for tone and emphasis.

Also, make sure that you do not say a visualisation too quickly for the participants to absorb. Practise saying it slowly, leaving silences so that they have time to do what you have requested. For example, if you have asked them to visualise being surrounded by a sphere of coloured light, wait for a few moments for them to see or sense this happening. Similarly, if you have told them that they will receive a message, a symbol, a gift or something else, wait for an appropriate period of time for it to manifest. If you have left them talking to or receiving messages from a higher being, be silent for a few minutes to enable them to communicate with the being. In this situation, you may like to say that you will leave them to talk to their being for two/three/four minutes, so that they know you will not be moving on quickly. They will then know that they will have some time with their being and, therefore, they will be more relaxed.

A visualisation comes alive and is memorable when it is described in detail, using all the senses, some examples are below:

- See the beautiful gold, red, pink and purple hues on the white fluffy clouds during this magnificent sunset.
- Hear the mighty roar of the fresh sparkling waterfall.
- Smell the welcoming aroma of home cooking.
- Touch the pitted bark of the huge, old, oak tree and sense its wise energy.
- Taste the pure, sweet nectar as you drink it from the passion flower.

You also need to be aware of how some participants may feel when they are put in certain circumstances. If they are afraid or allergic to certain situations that you put them in, it will have a detrimental effect. Some examples are below:

- Some people are afraid of water, so, if you are leading them into the sea, a lake or a river, you need to give them some options that they will feel comfortable with. These options can be something like swimming in the pure, clear water or remaining safe on the shore absorbing the high-vibrational energy of the water.

- Others are afraid of heights or feel claustrophobic in small spaces. Here you need to emphasise that they are totally safe and that the higher beings are surrounding them and protecting them, or give them other options, as with the water example above.

- People who suffer from hay fever may produce symptoms if, for example, you lead them into a garden full of scented flowers. So emphasise that the air is clear and pure.

To prepare a visualisation:

- Decide the purpose of the visualisation and what you would like your participants to achieve, e.g. to meet a being of the higher realms, to find their life purpose or to release unwanted energies.

- Choose a journey that will fulfil the aim of your visualisation.

- Think of a starting place for your journey, e.g. a tranquil forest with a carpet of beautiful bluebells on the ground.

71

- Work out an ending for your visualisation and, if possible, come back to where you started, as this helps with grounding. However, you may return to a different place, but be vigilant and make sure that everyone is grounded when you finish.

- Write your journey down using bullet points as memory joggers. Make sure that you relax, ground, protect and raise energies at the beginning of the visualisation; and bring the participants slowly back into their physical bodies, ground them and thank the beings for their help at the end of the visualisation. You may also protect them at the close of the visualisation, even if you feel it is only for one person's benefit.

- Practise saying your visualisation, making sure you are speaking loudly and clearly.

- Say your visualisation with a relative or friend and obtain their honest feedback.

Example of a Visualisation – Meeting a being from the higher realms
Before you start, explain to your group that this visualisation will help them to connect with the higher realms by meeting an angel, spirit guide, fairy, etc. Ask them to make sure that they are sitting comfortably with straight backs and arms and legs uncrossed. Also, tell them that it will last for about 15 minutes.

- Close your eyes and take some really deep breaths. On the out breath, breathe out all unwanted energies from your physical body, such as anxiety, stress and anger. Feel the tension dissipating and your muscles relaxing as these energies leave you.

- Ground yourself by visualising your roots growing from your feet and exploring deep within the earth. Connect with Mother Earth and sense her warm, nurturing energy.

- Protect by visualising a pure, bright, purple sphere of light surrounding you with its spiritual energy, giving you a wonderful safe haven. Purple is a deeply spiritual colour.

- Now visualise a column of pure-white, high-vibrational, shimmering light coming to you through the purple sphere. Breathe it in and see it spread to every single cell of your being, so that you are radiant with the brilliant white light. Feel your energies being raised.

- You now find yourself in a beautiful place in nature. It may be a place that you know or a place in your imagination. See the beautiful colours of the trees, plants and wildlife. Feel the texture of some leaves. Hear the cheerful birdsongs and the wind in the trees. Use all your senses to get to know this place and take in the abundant beauty that surrounds you.

- You now realise that you are not alone. Who is with you? Is it an angel, maybe a fairy or possibly a spirit guide? How do you sense their energy?

- Connect with the being. What are they like? What are their feelings?

- Communicate with them by asking questions and letting them pop ideas into your head in the form of thoughts, pictures or, possibly, words. I will leave you for three minutes to get to know your higher being.

- (After three minutes). Your being gives you a gift. What is it? What meaning does it have for you? If you are not sure, ask them.

- Thank them for the present and also for presenting themselves to you.

- Bring yourself back to the meeting room and feel your chair beneath you. Become aware of your normal breathing.

- Feel your feet on the floor and connect with the earth again through your roots.

- Wiggle your fingers and toes, open your eyes and have a stretch.

- Spend a few moments in silence thinking about your visualisation: who you met, how you felt, what you sensed and what you received from the being.

After the visualisation, make sure that everyone is grounded by observing their mannerisms and, in particular, by looking into their eyes. If you are not sure, ask them if they feel OK. If they are not fully back into their body, ground them straight away before you continue with anything else.

To obtain the full benefit of the visualisation, your participants should reflect and consolidate their experiences, so you need to give them time to do this. You can ask them to share and talk about the visualisation or tell them to do an activity about it. Another way is to have a break immediately after the visualisation, which will have grounding benefits, but you must make sure that they talk about, and so reflect on, their visualisation.

To share a visualisation:

- If you have a small group, you can ask people to share, in turn, by talking about their experiences of the visualisation.

- With a medium-sized group, you can ask them to pair up and take it in turns with their partner. If you have an odd number of participants, you will need to partner somebody – obviously this is not needed if there is an even number of people in the group.

- If you have a large group, you can ask people to form smaller groups of three or four and take it in turns to talk about their experiences within their group. When you convene back into the large group, you may like to ask them if they would like to share one or two interesting or remarkable experiences with the whole group.

- If you have a break immediately after the visualisation, you may like to ask the group not to speak about the visualisation during the break but to share their experiences after they have been refreshed.

Preparing and running activities will be discussed in the next chapter, but activities that serve to consolidate the experiences of a visualisation include:

- Drawing something from the visualisation and then sharing the drawings with others, if you feel that it is appropriate.

- Writing about the experiences of the visualisation and then sharing these, if you feel people would be happy doing this.

- Using a pack of spiritual cards by spreading the pack face down on the floor or splaying them in your hands with the pictures facing you and asking each person to take a card that they feel drawn to. If you ask your higher beings for help, the cards usually have relevance to your participants' visualisations. You can ask your participants to share their experiences, if you feel it is appropriate.

- Using the information gained from the visualisation to lead into the next session. For example, after visualising meeting a higher being, the next session could be writing to the higher being.

Please remember that your participants do not have to share and they are perfectly entitled to keep their encounters private. If they do not share, it is important that they either draw or write about their experiences. This helps them to reflect on their visualisation and gives them a record of their experiences.

Examples of More Visualisations
These examples explain the main visualisation; however, if using or adapting them, please remember to relax, ground, protect and raise energies at the beginning and bring people back slowly, as well as remembering to ground them, at the end.

Cleaning your Aura with Higher Beings
- You find yourself in a beautiful flower garden on a bright, sunny day. Look among the flowers and take in the depth of their colours and the sweet aromas of the pure, clear fragrances.

- You now notice some higher beings standing by a tree. They beckon to you and ask you to come near them. As you do, you feel their loving warm energy sweeping around you.

- They ask you to stand in the middle of a beautifully manicured, green chamomile lawn and tell you they are going to cleanse your aura. As you stand on the lawn, the scent from the chamomile leaves feels calming and relaxing. Take some deep breaths.

- Now you see shafts of sparkling coloured light coming towards you and the higher beings start weaving beautiful patterns just outside your aura with the light. There are so many wonderful shimmering colours glistening in the sunlight.

- The higher beings connect their hearts with yours and you feel the love they are sending to you. Open your heart to receive their love. Feel the beauty and purity of their energy, their delight at being able to work with you and their joy that you are open to receive their love and assistance. All they want to do is help you.

- You are now surrounded by a sphere of beautiful, patterned, coloured light and you sense it gently healing, purifying, absorbing unwanted energies, breaking up blockages and strengthening your aura.

- The higher beings are forming a circle around you and the sphere of light. They are stroking the light sphere and pulling out the unwanted energies. You feel your aura becoming clear, pure and shining with bright beautiful colours. You are also left with a deep sense of peace. I will leave you for a while, so that the higher beings can do their work and you can enjoy the beautiful coloured light, while feeling wonderfully peaceful.

- The coloured sphere of light slowly dissipates, leaving your aura filled with all the potentials for your good, your growth and your health. You feel the joy that this clarity brings you, your emotions are clear and free, your body is serene and strong and you are connected to your path of spiritual growth.

- Thank the higher beings for what they have just done for you. Say goodbye and return.

Healing in the Clouds

- You find yourself walking effortlessly up a small mountain. There is a gravel path with deep, lush grass either side. There are a few small green trees that look like islands in the grass.

- On the way, you walk through a white cloud that is encircling the mountain. Eventually you come out of the cloud into brilliant sunshine and you are surprised to find just the top of the mountain peeking above the perfect circle of cloud.

- As you look across the top of the cloud, you notice angels around the edge of the cloud protecting you.

- Now the surface of the cloud seems to change and you see your higher beings walking on top of it. They beckon for you to join them. You trust them and step onto the cloud. You are surprised to find that it easily takes your weight.

- What is the surface of your cloud like? If it is smooth and slippery you can skate with your higher beings. If it is like snow you can play cloud balls. If it has the texture of grass you can play football or volleyball with a ball made from the cloud. Play and have fun with your higher beings for a few minutes. Let all your worries and anxieties be drawn into the cloud where they are transmuted to neutral or positive energies. As you play and laugh on the cloud, you are being healed.

- Your higher beings are now taking you back onto the mountain. When you reach the mountain, the surface of the cloud changes back to its original form.

- Say goodbye to your higher beings. Walk back down the mountain, through the cloud, to the bottom where you started.

To Find your Sacred Inner Space

- You find yourself on the edge of a meadow, which is full of tall yellow grass. Notice how the grasses are moving together and forming waves in the gentle, pure breeze.

- Before you is a narrow path through the long grass which leads to a wood. The wood looks dark from where you stand, but you can see a brilliant aura surrounding it.

- Start walking towards the wood. Enjoy the walk and look out for animals, butterflies and birds.

- Soon you are standing in front of the thick, dark-green wood and, for a moment, there seems no way in. Pause for a while and wait until your eyes see an opening within the trees.

- When you see the opening, there is someone waiting for you. They may be one of your spirit guides, your guardian angel or another higher being. They may look human, angelic, fairy or animal. They are there to guide you to your sacred inner space. Introduce yourself and ask them their name. Take the first name that comes into your head.

- Now walk on with your guide into the wood. Smell the wonderful scent from the trees and notice the ground beneath your feet has changed from grass to soft, earthy, grounding layers of leaves, but you can still make out the path.

- Now look at the many trees and sense their different, mighty, wise energies.

- It is not long before you find yourself in a small clearing. There are gentle beams of light pouring in from the sky above the treetops. They may be moonbeams, sunbeams or even starlight. Stand and look around the clearing for a moment taking it all in.

- In the centre you see three large standing stones. Go and touch them to feel their energies and then sit down between them. You feel very safe and that you belong in this place.

- As well as the energy from the stones, you become aware of the energies from the grounding motherly earth and also the spiritual high-vibrational sky. After a while, you become aware that the energy from the earth beneath you and the sky above you meet here. Enjoy the merging of these energies within you and spend some time here, as this is your sacred inner space.

- It is now time to go. Let your guide take you back to the edge of the wood. Thank your guide and anybody else that you may have met.

- Walk back along the path through the tall grass. Do you notice different animals, butterflies or birds this time? Be aware that you can go back to your sacred inner space whenever you want.

Leading Meditations

When leading a meditation, explain to your participants what you will be focusing on and the benefits of stilling the mind, as well as what it can do for them. You also need to say that you will open the meditation by guiding them to open up to the higher energies in a safe way. Then you will be silent for the number of minutes that you feel this meditation needs, after which you will bring them back gently and safely again.

An excellent way to meditate is by focusing on breathing. There are many variations of meditating with the breath, but some of the most common for spiritual meetings are concentrating on normal breathing or breathing in positive energy and breathing out negative energy, which helps relaxation, as our muscles can unwind more effectively when they are not clogged with unwelcome energies. A lovely way to meditate with the breath combined with raising energies is to focus on breathing in positive energy and breathing out love, peace, joy or any other positive quality to the world.

Example of a Meditation – Using the breath
To follow is an example of counting numbers while meditating with the breath. Begin by explaining that your students may lose count or their mind may wander, but this is fine and normal. Tell them to just start again and not judge themselves.

- Breathe deeply in and, as you breathe out, release all unwanted energies from your physical body. As these energies leave you, sense your muscles relaxing. Gently let go and empty your mind.

- Take your attention to the bottom of your feet and visualise roots growing deep into the earth. Connect with Mother Earth and sense her wonderful energies.

- Protect yourself by visualising a form of protection that you resonate with all around you. (Only use this protection for experienced meditators).

- Sense a higher being with you sending you love to help you raise your energy vibrations.

- Breathe deeply in, counting from 1 to 5: 1 - 2 - 3 - 4 - 5 (say the numbers slowly).

- Release the breath counting from 1 to 5: 1 - 2 - 3 - 4 - 5 (again say the numbers slowly). Do not force your breathing; just let it flow naturally.

- I will let you continue doing this in your own time for about 10 minutes.

- (After 10 minutes) Bring your attention back into the room and feel yourself sitting on your chair.

- Ground yourself by sensing your roots growing down from the bottom of your feet and deep into the earth again. Feel the energy of our earth through your roots and ground yourself.

- When you are ready, wiggle your fingers and toes and open your eyes.

- How do you feel?

Example of a Meditation – Focusing on a candle
- Take your attention to the bottom of your feet and grow some beautiful strong roots into the earth. Let them connect with the earth, sense her wonderful energy and ground yourself with her.

- Be aware of a pure high-vibrational crystal light surrounding and engulfing you. Know that only the highest and purest energies can come through this light to you, so you are protected.

- Breathe deeply in and fill your physical, emotional and mental bodies with the revitalising high-vibrational energy. As you slowly breathe out release all anxiety, problems and tension. Sense these unwanted energies leaving you and, as they go, feel your muscles relaxing and be aware of sinking deeper into your chair.

- Now focus your gaze on the flame of the candle and meditate on it. I will guide you back in 10 minutes' time.

- (After 10 minutes, say the following softly and slowly). Slowly bring your attention back into this room.

- Feel the chair beneath you.

- Feel your feet on the floor and grow your roots down into Mother Earth and ground yourself with her again.

- When the time is right, wiggle your fingers and toes, open your eyes and have a stretch.

When ending a meditation you should make sure everybody is grounded and has time to reflect on their experiences in the same way as discussed for ending visualisations. People will not consciously experience as much with meditation as they do with visualisation; but, because the mind is stilled to a greater extent with meditation, they will usually receive more benefits over time.

CHAPTER FIVE

SPIRITUAL ACTIVITIES

By the end of Chapter Five you will:

- Know how to run an activity

- Have a selection of different types of activities you may like to use

Running Spiritual Activities

Activities create variety in a spiritual programme which enhances the participants' experience and understanding, as well as introducing the spiritual subject matter to their physical realms. Activities can also help to raise the energies of the group, and so are especially beneficial after a meal break, visualisation or meditation, when energies tend to be lower. Also, if during your meeting it looks like your participants' energy levels are low, e.g. if people are yawning, then run an activity to raise their vibrations.

There are an infinite number of activities that may be done during spiritual meetings which can augment your information. For example, drawing scenes or beings from visualisations or meditations you have just run, singing related songs or using appropriate spiritual cards. Also, you may have your own unique gifts and talents that you can use, such as acting, a therapy, yoga etc. If you are using your own skills where there may be an element of risk to participants, as in the use of aromatherapy oils with potential contra-indications or the possibility of injury when doing yoga, make sure that you are insured for this skill before introducing it as an activity to your group.

Generally, an activity should not be like a visualisation or meditation, in that it should not involve visiting other realms of existence or having one's eyes closed for long periods, unless it is a healing activity. This is because it will not provide the variety or energy boost a spiritual meeting needs.

When presenting an activity to your group, always try to explain it as simply and positively as possible, and never say that you think it may be a bit complicated or difficult, as this sows the seeds of uncertainty and, if they are not confident, they may feel that they cannot do it.

To introduce an activity to your group:

- First, briefly explain the activity in one sentence and give the outcome or benefits, if relevant, so that people have a brief overview and, hopefully, a feeling of excitement and a desire to experience it.

- Then explain it with as much detail as you can, which may mean breaking it down into stages. If there are many stages, you may want to write them on a flip chart or provide handouts to help people remember what to do next.

- Look around your group and check to make sure they understand what you want them to do. If they do not understand, explain it again, but make sure that you do this in a different way.

- Do the activity immediately after your explanation while it is fresh in their minds.

When the activity is finished, and depending on what it was, it is usually best for participants to share their experiences in the same way as with visualisations and meditations.

Different Types of Activities

There are innumerable different interesting types of activities that can be used in spiritual meetings. To follow is a selection of a few that you may like to use; however, you can invent your own or alter or combine some of these to suit your needs.

Many activities require people to work in pairs, so if you have an even number of people you will be free to supervise; however, if you have an odd number in your group, then you must partner somebody as well as manage your group.

Working with Objects

1. Intuition with objects

Prepare the activity beforehand by gathering an object for each person in your group. To do the activity, explain that it will help to sharpen intuitive skills and then spread the items on the floor. Let each individual intuitively select an object they feel drawn to or put all the objects in a bag and let everybody pick one, at random, out of the bag without seeing it. Ask your participants to spend some time tuning into their object to help them receive impressions, messages or an idea of its past, and then share these, in turn, with the group. This kind of intuition with objects is called psychometry, and some examples of items you can use are below.
Pebbles
Seashells
Flowers, plants or bulbs (these can be taken home and planted)
Pictures of higher beings
Pictures of butterflies, birds, animals etc.

2. Intuition with personal objects

This activity is similar to *Intuition with objects,* only people put a personal possession, such as a piece of jewellery or pen etc., into a bag without others seeing. Explain that this activity will help to enhance intuition and, additionally, tell your participants that it must be done in a sensitive way with respect for the feelings of others, because some personal information may surface. Each individual then takes an item from the bag, without other people seeing what they have taken, and tunes into it to receive some perceptions. If a person selects their own object, they must put it back into the bag and choose another one. When everybody has chosen an object, each person reveals their article and shares their impressions with the group, including who they think the object belongs to, and then the article is returned to its owner.

3. Putting a quality into an object

Tell your participants that this activity can help to raise their energies and that of others. Give each course participant an object or ask them to intuitively select one. For examples of objects to use, look at the *Intuition with objects* activity on the previous page. Ask your group members to focus on a quality, such as love, peace, joy, health etc., and project it into the article by holding it in their hands and concentrating on putting the energy of the quality into it. Participants can then take their object home and place it somewhere significant so that the quality radiates to all who are there. Alternatively, they may like to place it somewhere meaningful, such as in a shopping centre, near a school or hospital etc. to spread the energies to more people.

Working with Energy

1. Feeling your own aura

This activity is good to do after you have given your group some information about auras, as it will help them to be sensitive to the different layers of their own aura. Ask your participants to rub their hands together and then hold them as far apart as possible, with palms facing each other. Next, ask them to slowly bring their palms together until they feel a tingling or repelling sensation, a feeling of touching a slightly deflated bouncy ball, heat or cold. Everybody feels it differently; but, however they sense it, reassure them that they are feeling a layer of their aura. Next, tell them to push their hands through this barrier, which will feel a little weird (like sticky toffee or very tingly), and see if they can find another layer. If they continue, depending on how far their hands are apart, they may be able to find a third layer.

2. Perceiving the auras of others

There are a number of interesting ways that people can learn to be perceptive of the auras of others:

- Ask your participants to find a partner and stand on opposite sides of the room from each other. Partner A should stand still while partner B rubs their hands together and, with the palms of their hands facing partner A, walk towards them, concentrating on perceiving their aura. Partner B should notice the subtle sensations of partner A's aura, which can be a tingling feeling, a feeling of heat or cold or some kind of resistance especially when they enter the different layers. Then ask partner A and partner B to change roles.

- You will need some paper, coloured crayons and something to lean on, like a clipboard, for each participant. Ask your participants to find a partner, sit facing each other and perceive the other person's aura. When they are ready, tell them to draw the colours of the aura that they see or sense around their partner. If they do not see anything, ask them to meditate on what colour is there and then draw this.

- In a group situation, sit against a plain background with your group members looking straight at you. Ask your participants to defocus their eyes and look at your nose. With a little time, they should be able to see the bright etheric layer of your aura around your head. Tell them that if they view it directly it will disappear. As they share their observations, ask them to continue looking and the colours of the emotional layer may become visible. If you have time, you may like to invite others to sit on the chair for their aura to be viewed, but do not force people to do this.

3. **Perceiving the auras of nature**
   Take your group outside, if you are able, and ask them to look at the auras of flowers, trees, insects and animals. The auras of trees are especially large in the springtime, when they are bursting with life. The group's findings can be discussed while you are still outside or you may like everybody to share when you return to your room. Being outside observing nature has a grounding effect and it helps people to get in touch with the natural world. However, if you do not have access to an outside area you can use pot plants and domestic animals.

4. Ruffling and stroking the aura

Explain to your group that ruffling the aura will energise them and when their aura is stroked it will calm and ground them. Ask everyone in your group to find a partner. With partner A standing still, partner B starts at their feet and, working up to the head, makes quick, light, upward movements using both hands mixing the layers of the aura together. Ask them to continue ruffling the aura completely around partner A. This can have an ungrounding effect for some people, so tell partner A that if they feel faint, dizzy or in any way unwell, while this is being done to them, they must ask partner B to stop. You should then make sure that they are regrounded.

When the aura has been fully ruffled, ask partner B to stroke partner A's aura gently and carefully downwards around them, from head to toe, doing each layer in turn, working from nearest to the physical body outwards. This should have a soothing, calming and grounding effect. When they have discussed experiences, they change over.

5. Sensing chakras

This activity will makes people aware of the subtle energies of chakras and is ideal to do just after you have given some information about chakras. Ask your participants to work in pairs. Partner A lies down on the floor and is made comfortable with pillows etc. Ask partner B to run a hand through the chakras from head to toe, in the emotional layer of the aura of partner A. They should sense the energies of the large chakras as they pass their hand through them. If not much is felt with that hand; try using the other hand, as each hand varies in sensitivity, which does not follow right- or left-handedness.

Next, ask them to feel the chakras in the other auric layers and note the different sensations. Let them both talk about where there may be possible chakra blockages, and then they swap over.

Working with Sound

1. **Singing "aah"**
Inform your participants that the sound of "aah" helps to open the heart chakra. Stand in a circle with your group and hold hands. Ask everyone to raise their hands at the same time and sing "aah" at least three times, raising their hands each time it is sung. Afterwards, share any sensations that may have been felt in the heart chakra area. This activity can be varied by letting group members take it in turns to stand in the middle of the circle and have "aah" sung to them. The effect on individuals can be uplifting and often emotional.

2. **Singing "om"**
This activity is done in exactly the same way as singing "aah", only "om" is sung. "Om" is said to be the first sound of the universe and can raise our energy vibrations when chanted.

3. **Sound exercise**
Sound has a profound effect on our emotional and mental well-being, as this activity demonstrates. You will need different kinds of music on CDs or electronic storage as well as a music player. Play some music and ask your participants to move to the sounds and sense it inside them creating the bodily movements. After a few minutes, play some completely different music, e.g. from meditative to drumming music, and ask your participants to note the change in their feelings and movement.

4. Singing songs

This is a great activity to help raise energy levels. You will need CDs or electronic storage, a music player and song sheets for each participant with words to well-known positive songs. Choose a song that most people will know and can easily be sung. For example, 'I Have a Dream' by Abba for an angel meeting and 'Imagine' by John Lennon for awareness of world energies. Give people a song sheet, stand in a circle, turn on the music player and sing along with the song.

5. Toning

You will need to explain that toning can change energy vibrations and help people to emotionally express themselves. Toning is holding the intention of producing the perfect sound. You may ask the higher beings to help you fulfil a purpose, which may be for healing, balancing chakras, unlocking certain aspects of consciousness, bringing in a higher being's energy or creating peace.

As an example of toning with the intention of bringing peace to the world, ask your group to stand in a circle and relax, especially the throat, lips and jaw. Ask the higher beings that you are working with to help you. Tell everyone to focus on a peaceful world, what this really means and would be like. Then ask the group to open their mouths and allow the sound to come through that feels right for them. Continue for as long as you have arranged, which is usually around three to five minutes.

Working with Colour

1. **Sensing the energy of different colours**
   This activity will help your group participants to become aware of the subtle energies of colour. Ask your participants to sit or stand in a circle and visualise being surrounded by a particular colour. Tell them to breathe it in to the cells of their being and taste, smell and really sense it. They should note how they feel, their posture and their attitude and then let the colour drain from them into the earth.

   Repeat with further colours that you wish them to experience and make them aware of how quickly colour can change their mental and emotional state.

2. **Dancing with colour**
   Dancing with colour is similar to *Sensing the energy of different colours*, but you play some appropriate music and ask your participants to dance while visualising a particular colour filling their physical and subtle bodies. Let them experience further colours and note the difference in the dance movements with each individual colour.

Drawing Activities

When you ask some people to draw a picture they immediately say that they cannot draw, they have not drawn anything since they were at school or have some other excuse for not wanting to do it. Explain to them that this is not a drawing test and that their drawing is a representation, they will have a reminder of their activity to take home and, if appropriate, tell them the benefits of the activity. Usually, once they get busy with their drawing, they find that they enjoy it.

1. Drawing scenes from visualisations and meditations

After you have run a visualisation or meditation, and before you ask your group to share with one another, give each person some paper, coloured crayons and something to lean on, such as a clipboard. Then ask them to draw a scene from their visualisation or meditation. When all the drawings are complete, ask them to share their visualisation or meditation experiences, with their drawing being the focal point. They will then have the picture to take home with them to remind them of their visualisation or meditation.

2. Object drawing

Object drawing accesses information from the sub-conscious mind, because you ask people to draw certain objects together on a piece of paper without consciously knowing why they are doing it. This is an activity where you cannot initially explain too much detail, but you can inform them that it will give them insights into their life that they may not have thought about. It can also be a lot of fun as well as revealing.

Hand out paper, coloured crayons and something to lean on and ask your group to make a picture using four to eight objects that you want them to draw. When everybody has finished their drawings, check that they have all drawn the specified objects and take it in turns to share. It is best if the person who has done the drawing interprets their own picture, because we all have our personal understanding of life. For example, a bear may be viewed as a ferocious animal to some people but a cuddly object to others. However, if somebody is stuck, others can help by giving their recommendations.

There are some general meanings of objects, which may help with interpretation. In her book, *Transform Your Life,* Diana Cooper has a detailed list of representations for many objects. Most of the following meanings have been taken from her book:

- water (river, sea, pond etc.) – emotions – rough = emotional turmoil, calm = tranquility
- boat – a way through emotions – where has it come from and where is it going?
- bridge – a way over emotions – where does it lead?
- moon – feminine energy – gentle, nurturing aspect
- sun – masculine energy or happiness
- cloud – sadness – what is the cloud over?
- tree – life – is it bare or in full leaf?
- flower – creativity
- fence – a barrier or block that can be moved
- hedge – a barrier or block that is more difficult to move
- gate – an opportunity or a way through a situation
- path – life path – is it straight, twisty, smooth or bumpy?
- house – how you represent yourself – welcoming, homely, modern, old-fashioned?
- animal – your characteristics – same as those of the animal
- person – usually a representation of you
- vehicle – how you make your way through life – fast, slow etc.
- a higher being – your good qualities – same as those of the being

When interpreting the meaning of an object, see if it is smaller or bigger compared to the size of other images on the page. For example, if a drawing of a person is comparatively small on the page, they may be timid or lack confidence. Look at where objects are drawn on the page, as the left represents the past, the middle symbolises the present and the right is for the future. Also look at the colours that have been used. The universal meanings of colours are below:

Red – energy and vitality

Pink – love

Orange – sociable, friendly, positive ambition

Gold – wisdom

Yellow – thought

Green – balance, love of nature, inner peace

Spring green – new beginnings, healing

Turquoise – communication, honesty

Blue – loyal, genuine

Deep blue – peaceful, trustworthy, mental healing

Purple – spiritual, healing abilities

Black – unknown, mysterious

Brown – earthiness, solid, dependable, physical, practical

Grey – sadness, confusion

It is beneficial to have some experience of helping people with their drawings, so do this activity with friends or family before you introduce it in a meeting. It can be great fun.

Healing Activities

You will need to have experience of healing before running the *Simple healing* and *Colour Healing* activities.

1. Simple healing

Decide what sort of healing you wish to do, e.g. spiritual or angel healing. For general spiritual meetings and courses, emphasise that this is a short taster session of five to 10 minutes long and not a full treatment.

Ask your participants to find a partner and decide who is to receive and who is to give healing first. Partner A, who is going to receive healing first, sits in a chair. If they have a back problem, ask them to sit either sideways or to straddle the chair (with the chair back against their chest) and lean on a cushion or pillow for comfort so that their partner can easily reach their back.

Start the session by making sure everybody is grounded and protected and then invite the healing energy you are working with to come in for everyone's highest and greatest good. Partner B places their hands on the shoulders of partner A for a few moments to get used to partner A's energies and for partner A to get used to partner B's energy. This also helps to ground partner A.

Partner B starts the healing by placing their hands on partner A's body or just above it in their aura. The usual procedure for a meeting situation is to start at the head and work down the body. Tell your participants that if they are placing their hands on the physical body, the touch must be very light and no pressure of any kind should be exerted. The cycle of energy can often be felt when the hands are first applied to a position. When this energy cycle has receded, or when they intuitively feel that it is right, slowly raise the hands so that they are also sending healing energy to the layers of the aura and then move on to the next hand position. With intimate, tender areas or wounds, participants must only work in the aura.

To finish, ask partner B to stroke the aura of partner A so that it is smooth and not 'ruffled up'. Then thank the higher energies for their help and make sure everybody is grounded again. Ask partner B to wash their hands to detach from partner A's energies and tell everyone to have a drink of water. Give them time to talk about their experiences before they swap over.

2. Colour healing
Colour healing is done in exactly the same way as *Simple healing*, only the person giving the healing visualises a particular colour flowing from their hands to their recipient. This can be a colour they intuitively feel is right or one that is given from you. However, if anyone is unsure about which colour is the best to use, choose white, as it contains all the colours.

3. Stroking and healing the auric layers
Ask your participants to find a partner and decide who is going to give and who is going to receive first. Partner A, who is receiving first, sits on a chair. Ground and protect everybody and ask the higher energies to give healing for the highest and greatest good of all. Partner B gently and slowly strokes the etheric layer of partner A all around them, from head to toe.

They then do the same for the emotional, mental and, finally, spiritual layers, working intuitively with the distance of the layers from the physical body, as this varies from person to person. When everybody has finished, ground them, ask partner B to wash their hands to detach from partner A's energies and make sure each member of the group has a drink of water. Then everyone shares their experiences and the partners swap over.

4. **Thank-you-for-health list**

   Tell your participants that we tend to focus on what is not working in our bodies, which can dominate our thoughts. Whatever we think about magnifies and we energise ill health by giving it attention. Alternatively, we can think about our body functioning well and obtain health and healing. Ask your group to make a list of their body parts that are comfortable, working well and helping them to live a good life. Then breathe deeply and focus on these parts of their body and thank them. Afterwards, ask them to share how they feel, taking it in turns to do so.

Psychic Activities

Psychic activities are a lot of fun, especially for children. The exercises and the laughter that ensues are some of the best ways to raise energy levels. Emphasise that this is light-hearted fun and people should not get disillusioned if intuitiveness is not one of their gifts or talents, as they will excel with another skill.

1. **Intuitiveness**

   Before you begin this activity, remind everyone about the confidence agreement that you put in place at the beginning of your meeting. Next, ask everyone to find a partner and tell partner A to close their eyes.

Partner B then breathes with partner A and looks at their physical and energetic bodies. After a few minutes, ask B to stop and A to open their eyes. Partner B can then tell partner A what they have picked up about them, and then they swap over.

2. Psychic colours

With your group divided into pairs, tell partner A to close their eyes. Ask partner B to think of a colour and then project this colour into the third eye chakra of partner A. After a couple of minutes tell them to stop, ask A to tell B what colour they were using, and swap over. Alternatively, you can hold a coloured piece of paper up to give all the partner B's the colour to use.

3. Psychic emotions

Ask everybody to think of something that made them happy and then think of something that made them sad. This can be kept private, as they do not have to tell anybody what it is. With everybody divided into partners A and partners B, partner A closes their eyes and either thinks of their happy or sad event. B then tells A whether they were thinking the happy or the sad occasion, and then they swap over.

4. Psychic movements

For this activity you will need another room available. The group should be divided into partners A and B. A goes to the other room where B cannot see them. A does a specific movement, such as scratches their nose or silently claps their hands, while B intuitively concentrates on what movement they are making. A then returns to the first room and B should try to mimic A's movements. They then swap.

5. Psychic awareness
Ask everyone to find a partner and partner A thinks of an action that they would like B to do, e.g. smile, raise an arm/leg, rock backwards and forwards or from side to side. A transmits this action to B's third eye chakra and visualises them doing it. See if B picks up on the energy of A's thoughts and does the action, and then they swap over.

6. Psychic awareness in a group
One person from the group goes out of the room. The group then decide on an action that they want the person to do when they come back to the room, e.g. skip, dance, hum, whistle, sing. Bring the person back into the room and visualise that person doing the action that was chosen. See if they pick up on the energy of the thoughts of the rest of the group and do the action. Each person takes it in turn to leave the room and pick up on the energy of the action required of them when they return.

Dowsing
Dowsing works by our inner knowing picking up information from the energy around us and relaying it to our subconscious mind. This, in turn, sends the information to our wrists, making unconscious muscle contractions that cause the dowsing instruments to move slightly, often to the surprise of our conscious mind.

Dowsing does not work for everybody, and, generally, if it does not work for somebody, it is because they do not need to dowse as they can intuitively sense the energies. If this happens, tell them to do the activity without using the dowsing instruments.

To run a dowsing activity, you need to be able to dowse so that you can demonstrate what is required. It is best to practise dowsing activities so that you are proficient before introducing them to others.

1. **To dowse an aura**

   Divide your group into pairs. You will need dowsing instruments, usually either pendulums or L rods, for each pair. Partner A stands still on one side of the room while partner B stands on the other side and sets the intention for the dowsing instrument to move in a certain way when it reaches the edge of the layers of partner A's aura. Partner B then moves towards partner A, noting where the layers in the aura are. This activity can also be done with plants.

2. **To discover the effect of electromagnetic energies on our auras**

   This activity is not only visible proof that man-made electromagnetic and microwave energies affect natural subtle energy fields, but also a reminder that higher beings can protect us. You will need dowsing instruments for each pair and you will need to ask your participants to use their mobile phones, but tell them that no calls will be made.

   In pairs, partner A stands still throughout this activity on one side of the room holding a mobile phone that is initially switched off. Partner B goes to the other side of the room and, by slowly walking towards partner A, dowses the edge of a layer of their aura and notes where the edge of the aura is by placing a stone or some kind of marker on the floor.

   Partner A turns on the mobile phone and partner B dowses the edge of the same layer of their aura again. Predictably, the aura should have shrunk.

Now ask partner A and partner B to call on the higher beings of your choice to protect partner A against the harmful electromagnetic and microwave energies of the mobile phone. Repeat the dowsing as before and the layer of partner A's aura should have expanded to a larger size than what it was when they first started. Partner A and partner B should then swap over.

3. **Finding chakra imbalances with a pendulum and balancing**
   Ask your participants to find a partner. You will need to have pendulum dowsers for each pair. Partner A lies on the floor and is made comfortable with pillows etc. Partner B swings the pendulum from side to side over a chakra in the emotional layer of the aura and then leaves it to make its own movement. If the pendulum makes a proper circle (it does not matter which way round), the chakra is in balance. If the pendulum does anything else, the chakra is out of balance. Repeat for all the large chakras down the body.

   To balance the chakras, ground and protect everybody and ask the higher or healing beings to help you. Tell partner B to hold their hands in the emotional layer of the aura over the relevant chakras, in turn, for as long as they feel is necessary, as follows:
   - One hand over the third eye and the other over the base.
   - One hand over the throat and the other over the sacral.
   - One hand over the heart and the other over the solar plexus.

Do not worry about the crown or other chakras, because if the main chakras down the body are in balance then the others should automatically be synchronised.

When everyone has finished thank the healing beings and check the chakras again with the pendulum. You may like to extend the activity for the mental and spiritual layers of the aura, and then the partners swap over.

Craft Activities
Craft activities take a lot of time and need a fair amount of preparation to source the craft materials. They are great for children's groups, but are not recommended for adult meetings unless it is advertised as a spiritual craft meeting, e.g. making angel Christmas cards. This is because most people will not expect to spend a long time on a craft activity, and they may feel the meeting is not what they anticipated, which will lead to disappointment. However, with craft activities, the participants will have something to take home with them to remind them of the meeting.

Examples of craft activities are making cards, bookmarks, collages, jewellery and decorating journals. To make wish cards, for example, you will need some white cardboard to make the cards and provide crayons, felt tips, pens, glue, paper shapes, glitter, feathers, beads etc. Ask your participants to think about what they would like to wish for and decorate the cards with this in mind using the materials. Then they write their dreams and wishes inside the card and then take it home after the meeting to enable it to radiate the energy of their wishes to them whenever they look at it.

Other General Spiritual Activities

1. **Walking in nature**
   For this activity, you will need access to somewhere outside, such as a garden, park or the countryside. Tell your participants to ask nature a question, then take a walk outside and obtain the answer through natural objects, which they can pick up and bring back with them for discussion afterwards.

2. **Thank-you walk**
   For this activity, take your participants outside and, as they walk, say 'thank you' mentally for things they see, hear, sense or experience. This usually has a grounding and invigorating effect on people. When you all convene, ask them how they feel.

3. **Expressing creativity**
   You will need to have some paper, coloured crayons and something to lean on. Ask your participants to decide on a quality that they would like to express, e.g. tranquillity, joy, aspiration, and focus on the quality to decide its colour, sound, smell, taste, shape, texture etc. Then express this on the paper and, when finished, spend some time looking at it. This is an expression of one of their aspects, and by drawing and looking at it they will be able to absorb the quality and express it in their life. Ask them to share their creation with the group if they want to.

4. **Thank-you list**
   Give your participants some paper, pens and something to lean on. Ask them to write down every blessing they have in their life, which should not only include material things, but guide them to think about their gifts and talents, situations, challenges, friendships, abundant water and food, body, senses,

love, higher beings and the natural world etc. When they have finished, ask them to breathe deeply and picture all the good things they have written down and say thank you for them. Discuss, in turn, how they now feel with the rest of the group.

5. Wishing

Tell your group to think of something they would like for the highest good of all. When more than one person holds the focus of a wish, it adds power and intensity, so it is helpful to do this activity in pairs or threes. First, ask your participants to discuss their wishes in their small groups until they all totally understand and are clear about what each person is asking for. Then give everyone a small object, such as a stone or feather, and ask them to take it in turns in their group to hold their small object in their hands and say their wish. It can be said aloud or to themselves. Everybody in the small group then concentrates on the wish, visualising the person or subject of the wish having it, being it or doing it. Share any feedback, and then the next person has their turn. Participants can take their object home with them and put it in a suitable place to radiate the energy of the wish into the environment and to others who are there.

6. Spiritual cards

You will need a pre-bought pack of spiritual cards, preferably with a picture and a little bit of writing on the face. Before use, cleanse the cards by asking the higher beings that you resonate with to clear the unwanted energies from the deck or by lightly tapping on the top of the cards while holding the intention to release all lower energies and raise the cards to a higher vibration.

There are a number of ways cards may be used in a group situation, but the easiest method is to shuffle the cards and ask your participants to think of a question or a request for help while you splay the cards, picture-side down, on a table or the floor. Ask your participants to pick a card that draws their attention by running their hand a few centimetres above the cards. They may notice a change in energy, such as heat, cold or tingling, when their hand is above a certain card, or they may use their intuition.

Ask each person to read the writing on their card or interpret the picture. To understand the meaning of a picture, ask them to look at an object in the drawing that attracts their eye and take any messages that come into their mind. These messages will always be correct. They may find that a few objects attract their eye, if so, tell them to look at each one in turn until they receive a message for all of them. If you have a small group they can share their findings, in turn, with the whole group, but if your group is large you can ask people to pair up or go into groups of three to four to share their findings.

Some people may have chosen a card that is the wrong way up. This indicates that there is resistance or a blockage in that area.

Another lovely way to work with cards in a group is to ask people to work in pairs, and as soon as they have picked a card, give it to their partner before they look at it and then they read each other's card in turn.

CHAPTER SIX

HOW WE LEARN

By the end of Chapter Six you will:

- Know some of the different ways that people learn

- Be able to use some techniques for memorising information in your meetings

- Have an idea of different teaching tools

Learning Aspects

Teaching with your Participants' Learning in Mind

Understanding how your participants learn is a key feature of teaching. Perceptions about learning have changed over recent years, from the old notion that the teacher stands in front of rows of students giving out information while they sit still, face the front and have their heads filled with knowledge. We now know that we can learn quicker and memorise more if we get some personal experience with the information, can talk about it with others and are able to reflect on it afterwards.

Your participants will learn and remember more if they are comfortable and relaxed; achieving this is explained in Chapter Two in the *Making People Feel Welcome* section and in Chapter Three in the *Presentation and Caring for your Group* section.

The session should be broken down into parts and not be one long ramble. It will help to raise expectations as well as aid relaxation if you explain the different parts you are going to teach at the beginning of your meeting when you are talking about the content.

For example, for a meeting designed around some particular higher beings, the parts could be:

- Describing and connecting with the higher beings.
- How the higher beings help us.
- Healing with the higher beings.

After you have made your participants welcome and opened the session, as described in Chapters 2 and 3, give your group some information about the first part. A higher degree of remembering is achieved by giving students a quick overview first, so that they have an idea of what to expect before more facts are provided. When they have all the detailed information, let them ask questions to make sure they fully understand it before you do something with it, like an activity, visualisation, meditation or a combination of these. Help them to share and reflect on their experiences and give them as much positive feedback as possible. It improves the flow of the meeting to separate the parts by having a break before you move on to the next part.

Your students will also learn more if you help them to have an awareness of what they can achieve from your meeting, e.g. to be able to receive messages from higher beings. This can also be incorporated at the beginning of your meeting when you inform them about the content.

Learning Using our Senses
We mainly learn by using three of our senses: sight, hearing and touch. Unless we are training in an occupation that uses the senses of smell or taste, e.g. an aromatherapist, perfumer or cook, we do not normally use these senses for learning. Everyone uses a mix of sight, hearing and touch for learning, but most people

find they have a dominant sense and use the other two senses to a lesser degree. Some people find that they use different senses in different circumstances and sometimes the dominant sense that we use for learning changes as we get older.

- People with the dominant learning sense of sight are visual learners. They need pictures, charts and diagrams with lots of colour, because colour is a great memory jogger. They like to look at the written word and benefit from having books, manuals and leaflets. Visualisations and meditations are great memory aids for visual learners.

- People who learn mainly by hearing are auditory learners. They like to listen to the spoken word to gain information. When they are reading, they learn better by speaking the words to themselves, and so they benefit from making tapes and listening to their own voice. And, of course, auditory learners benefit when you articulate your information.

- Individuals who prefer hands-on learning are tactile learners. They prefer to physically touch and experience the subject, so they benefit from doing activities in a course situation.

Unfortunately, we unconsciously like to teach using the sense that dominates our own learning abilities, and we must be mindful that others may need to learn in a different way. Therefore, when we plan our meetings we must provide a good ratio between giving information, visualisation or meditation and activities.

Think for a few moments about your own learning preferences:

- If you like maps, colourful drawings, charts, diagrams or cartoons then your dominant learning sense is visual.

- If you enjoy lectures, prefer to listen to tapes and CDs of the spoken word or regularly listen to the words of music then your dominant learning sense is auditory.

- If you are a practical person who likes to make things and has to touch something or take it apart to understand it better, then your dominant learning sense is tactile.

However, do not forget that we also take in information in the form of energy through our auras and chakras, which is a much more subtle form of learning.

Memorising

To learn efficiently, we need to be able to remember what we have learned so we can recall it at a later time. When people come to a meeting, the information that they have received in the past few minutes or hours will be stored in their short-term memory and they will be able to recall it fairly well during the time they are with you that day. However, if steps are not taken to transfer it to the long-term memory, they will probably have forgotten about 70% of it the following day. To help transfer as much information as possible to the long-term memory:

- Make sure your participants are relaxed, because this helps the parts of the brain that deal with retaining information work better.

- Use flip charts, boards, PowerPoint, leaflets or manuals with colourful writing, diagrams, lists, pictures or charts for visual learning. When writing the data, group it together or list it using bullet points, with each point in a different colour.

- Have visualisations, as these also help visual learners. It is especially beneficial for aiding memory retention if you ask your participants to see something silly.

- Do an activity, such as drawing, acting, dancing or something else, to do with your information, which is good for tactile learners.

- Talk and share information. This is good for auditory learners, especially if you make an important point by using a different accent, metaphors or by drawing on associations by using information your participants already know.

- Have frequent breaks.

- Use mnemonics. These are explained in the next section.

Mnemonics

Mnemonics help people to remember and recall information by translating the data into a form that the brain can retain better than when in its original form. Mnemonics are most often used to help students remember information for exams, but they are also useful memory joggers for all learning situations. To follow are some common forms of mnemonics, which can be adapted to fit many spiritual situations.

- Acronyms are words or phrases made up of the first letters of the data to be remembered. An example of a word that has already been used in this book for remembering what to do when closing a session is **PEG** – **P**rotect, **E**nergy awareness and **G**round. An example of a phrase that has already been used in this book to help remember what to do when opening a session is **G**reat **P**hysical **R**ealms – **G**round, **P**rotect and **R**aise energies.

- Rhymes or short poems are other good tools for remembering information. For example, '**R**ichard **O**f **Y**ork **G**ave **B**attle **I**n **V**ain' uses the first letter of each word to represent a colour of the rainbow – **R**ed, **O**range, **Y**ellow, **G**reen, **B**lue, **I**ndigo, **V**iolet. Examples of other common acronym rhymes are 'i before e except after c' to help with spelling, and '**N**ever **E**at **S**hredded **W**heat', to remember the compass directions in sequence – **NESW**.

- Music is an excellent tool to help people's memory, as a popular lyric can easily be put to a phrase or short poem. This is often used by companies to advertise their products – one of the most famous being Coca-Cola using the music to 'I'd Like to Teach the World to Sing'.

- Associations can help to aid memory. For example, to remember the directions of latitude and longitude: there is an '**N**' in longitude, so longitude runs **N**orth–South; therefore, latitude, which has no '**N**', must run East–West.

Mind Maps

Mind maps are great memory aids that present large amounts of information by setting it out in a clear, concise manner on one sheet of paper. Mind maps can also be used to bring information together from a number of individuals in the group and are especially good to help clarify data if it is confusing or complicated.

A mind map:

- Shows the connections between ideas in a visual way using keywords.
- Has a lot of information in one diagram on a single sheet of paper.
- Can be made to look attractive and humorous by using colours, symbols and pictures.
- Can be personalised to suit the participants.
- Encourages thinking, creativity, emotions and imagination.
- Can easily have information added to it.
- Can be fun to make in a group situation.
- Is a good aid to help people recall information.

Mind maps aid learning as well as help memory retention because they are visual and appeal to the visual learner. If you talk about the mind map as you make it on a flip chart or board it will appeal to the auditory learner and if you ask the participants for their input or if they physically add items to the mind map themselves it will appeal to the tactile learner.

The fundamental way to make a mind map is to only use keywords. A keyword is a phrase that has a maximum of three words, but often just one word, which reminds everyone of the whole item. To formulate a keyword, it is essential to take away all the unnecessary expressions and get to the basic meaning of each entry.

When making a mind map, use the paper with the longest side at the top (landscape), because there is more space for words, which run horizontally. Also, use different colours, symbols and pictures and do not to crowd too much into one corner or side.

To make a mind map, write a word or draw a picture or symbol for your topic in the centre of the paper. Then think of the main ideas associated with the topic and represent these with words, pictures or symbols and draw lines from them to the topic. Think further about it and add more ideas and draw lines or arrows to represent the connections between each idea, diverging outwards like the branches of a tree. You may also want to group some ideas together. At this stage you may want to start your mind map again, with your main ideas entered in a more orderly fashion. Then add further information with connecting lines and let it evolve until you have exhausted all your thoughts.

On the next page is a mind map about mind maps.

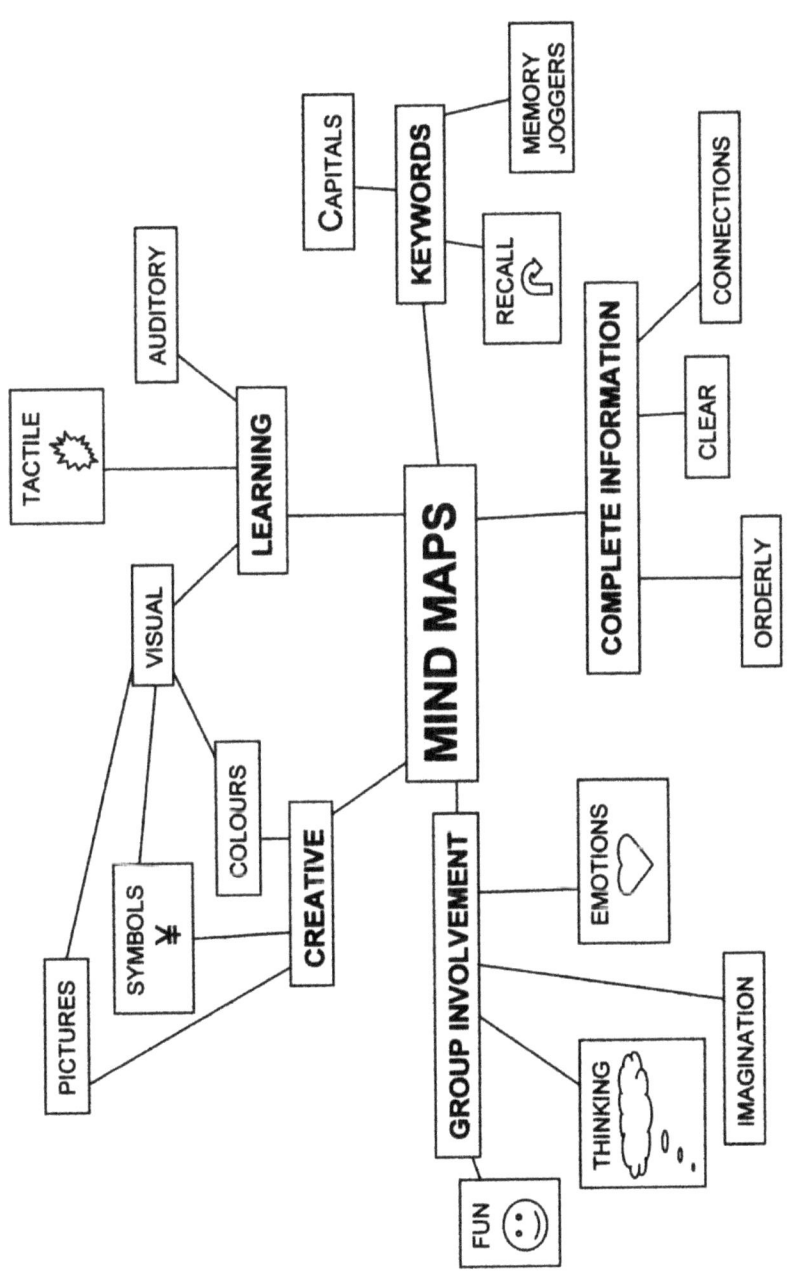

Music

It is great to have some low, soft music playing during your meeting, because music has a relaxing effect on people, while at the same time stimulating memory retention. It helps to synchronise the physical, emotional, mental and spiritual bodies, so harmonising the body and soul.

Music helps the whole brain become involved with the learning process, because the right hemisphere becomes involved with the music and the left hemisphere works with the information. This integrates the left and right hemispheres, which, in turn, increases learning and creative abilities.

When choosing music for your meeting, do so wisely. It is best to have pleasing, gentle music that people probably do not know and has no words, because the words of the music will clash with the words you are saying. A gentle rhythm is best and sharp noises, such as whale sounds, should be avoided. Be aware that people who are hard of hearing may find the music distracting, as your voice may merge with the music making it difficult for them to hear your words, so you may need to turn it off for the meetings that these people attend.

Teaching Tools

There are a number of different tools that can be used to help teaching and learning in a group meeting situation. To follow is a list of the main teaching tools.

Flip Charts

Flip charts are good for both preparing information beforehand as well as for use during the meeting. Flip chart pads have a large number of sheets which can hold a vast amount of information. Different coloured markers or flip chart pens can be used to make the information interesting as well as helping visual learners; however, do not use light colours, such as yellow or pastel shades, because these do not show up well and are difficult to read.

When using flip charts keep the information clear and simple, making sure that the text is large and tidy so that your participants can read it. Flip charts can be used to:

- Outline the content of the meeting at the beginning of the session, so that people know what to expect.

- Form the basic bullet points of your information. This also helps as a memory jogger for you so that you know what to talk about next.

- Outline an activity. You can keep the page up on the flip chart during the activity so that people can see what to do next.

- Review a session and collate feedback from the group, which helps to reflect on what has just been done and also helps to commit it to the long-term memory.

Blackboards or Whiteboards

One of the oldest tools is the blackboard, where information is written down on a blackboard with chalk either before or during the meeting. A more modern version is a whiteboard with coloured pens. Whiteboards are used in the same way as flip charts; however, once the space on the board is used up, it has to be rubbed out before further data can be added.

PowerPoint

PowerPoint is a good tool which can help to present information in the same way as flip charts, and a PowerPoint presentation can also look professional. PowerPoint presentations consist of a number of individual pages that are printed onto a plastic template or slide and projected onto a screen or thrown onto a screen from a projector linked directly to a computer. As the information is created on a computer the typed words are clear to read, which is helpful for long-term memory retention, particularly if it is colourful. If you use PowerPoint, you will need to be confident with computers and electrical equipment, as they can often be unreliable during meetings! Be aware that the hum of the fan in the projector can put some people off. Also, electrical equipment emits electromagnetic energy which is not compatible with our own subtle energy systems. This reduces the energy and size of our auras and, consequently, diminishes our connections with the higher realms, which is not good for spiritual meetings.

Notes and Manuals

It is impossible to remember everything from a meeting, so, having notes or manuals allows your participants to look something up at a later date. Also, people have something to take away from the meeting as a memento.

Notes and manuals help the visual learner, especially if there are pictures and diagrams with the information. As the notes and manuals have to be prepared beforehand, when you are compiling them only include the information that you intend to give out and do not include any activities, visualisations or meditations, as you will then have scope to change your programme during the meeting to adapt to your students' needs.

Other Teaching Tools
You may want to:

- Show a video or DVD.

- Invite a specialist to speak at your meeting, e.g. a sound healing therapist or a spiritual story teller.

- Have pictures or diagrams around your room displaying your subject matter. For example, hand positions for a healing session or pictures of different archangels for an angel meeting.

CHAPTER SEVEN

PUTTING TOGETHER A GOOD PROGRAMME

By the end of Chapter Seven you will:

- Know how to create a good timed programme

- Have examples of some spiritual programmes

Creating a Programme

Creating a good, smoothly running course takes many hours of preparation. Mark Twain is quoted as saying: "It usually takes me more than three weeks to prepare a good impromptu speech". As well as planning your meeting you should also rehearse it. At first you should do this by yourself, which is best done in front of a mirror so you can see how you come across. Then you can practise it with friends or family so they can give you constructive feedback. You can ask your higher beings to help you, but this should not be in place of your preparation, because, in my experience, higher beings help best if we put in our physical effort, so, with a good, well-balanced, rehearsed programme, their influence and guidance will make it a brilliant meeting.

When preparing your programme, you will need to have a timetable, and to do this you should have a rough idea of how long each item will take. However, no meeting is the same or runs exactly as planned, because participants and their numbers vary. Some people like to chat and ask a lot of questions, in which case you may find it challenging to present everything you had prepared, but if they are shy and reserved you will easily cover your programme and need more items to fill in the time.

Therefore, for each of the main parts of your meeting, you should give people the information and then have a number of activities, visualisations or meditations that you can use or leave out, depending on the time.

When you decide to run a spiritual meeting, you will probably already have some idea of the content and how you would like to present it. Now you need to think further and put all the elements together on a piece of paper. So get a blank sheet of paper and write down:

- The subject matter of your meeting.

- A title for your meeting. This should also be used in your advertising, so it should represent what you will be teaching and be catchy and interesting so that people will want to find out more.

- Who you hope will attend your meeting, e.g. children, adult beginners or people already on their spiritual path. If you are intending to run a course in the UK for children, the elderly or individuals who might otherwise be classed as vulnerable you must have a Disclosure and Barring Service (DBS) check which replaces the Criminal Records Bureau (CRB) check. The DBS check can be done online for a fee and takes from three to 10 working days to receive the results.

- What you would like your participants to achieve from your meeting. Also, write a positive statement and use it like an affirmation when preparing and running your programme. We discussed this in Chapter One on page 13.

- The time of day and how long you want to have your meeting, e.g. an evening, half day, whole day, one day or evening per week, one day or evening per month or a number of consecutive evenings or days.

- A date, start time, finish time, length and times of breaks including lunch if it is a day meeting. If you are hiring a venue the date will depend on when it is free.

- The main parts of your meeting, e.g. with a healing meeting the main parts could be: how healing works, giving healing to ourselves, giving healing to others.

- The number of activities, visualisations or meditations for each part, and list them in order of importance. Some will be included and some will not, depending on the time and the energy of your group.

- A timed programme. This will be explained in detail in the next section.

- A list of items that you will need, e.g. flip chart, flip chart pens, music player with music, paper, pens, crayons, clip boards, tea, coffee, sugar, milk.

Creating a Timed Programme

As explained before, to create a good programme you will need to have a mixture of:

- Talking – where you give out the information.

- Activities – those that you feel should be included and those that can be used as extras.

- Visualisations or meditations – which are usually included in your timed plan.

A meeting should never be less than 50% experiential, even if it does not go as planned. The experiential components are the activities, visualisations and meditations. However, do not include too many visualisations and meditations, because people can become ungrounded. Try to aim for a maximum of one short visualisation or meditation up to 15 minutes every 1.5 hours or a longer one every 2.5 hours.

You should have a number of grounding activities prepared that can be done between the visualisations and meditations. Grounding activities are more practical in nature and do not involve closing the eyes and connecting with higher energies.

You should also have some activities where participants interact with each other, especially at the beginning of your meeting, because this helps them to relax and removes tension. Encouraging interaction between your participants can be done by using ice-breakers, which was covered in Chapter Two. If you are holding a meeting over a day, you should have a grounding activity immediately after lunch, because people's energy is being used to digest their food and a visualisation or meditation at this time will send them to sleep. Also, try to end the meeting with a high-energy activity such as singing or movement, such as dancing.

If you have a large amount of information to give out, you should not talk for more than 20 minutes, because the brain stops absorbing information after this time. It is better to run a quick activity and then continue. When giving information, you can make it come alive and more interesting for your participants if you include short stories about your subject matter.

During your meeting, you should have your timetable with you and regularly consult it to ascertain whether you are running ahead or behind schedule, so that you know whether you need to add or leave out activities, visualisations or meditations. You can also quickly refer to your time table if you forget what comes next, and you may like to add some notes to it to use as memory joggers.

Make sure that you finish your meeting at the arranged time and do not overrun without asking if anybody needs to leave at that time. Also, do not say that the meeting has finished and then continue talking. Most people will expect to leave at the time you have stated.

After your meeting, you should spend some time reflecting on it. To do this, schedule a couple of hours no more than 24 hours after your meeting, while it is still fresh in your mind. Think how you felt it went? Could you have done more? Could you have reacted differently to a situation? Could you have said something different? Would there have been a different outcome if you had done or said something different? It helps to write these things down in a special reflective journal, so that you can look back on it before your next meeting. However, do not be too hard on yourself, because nobody is perfect or knows everything.

Examples of Timed Programmes

To follow are examples of programmes that you can adapt for your own meetings.

An evening programme of 2 hours to meet some higher beings

For adults who are already on their spiritual path.
Positive statement: My students connect brilliantly with the higher beings during and after my meeting.
Meet at 18.45 for a 19.00 start. Hand out name tags, give participants a hot drink, get people talking or let each person draw a spiritual card and say why they feel they have chosen this card.
19.00 Welcome talk to tell the participants:

- The main topics – Connecting with the higher beings, How the higher beings can help us.
- What they should get out of the meeting.
- Where the toilets are.
- The fire procedures (if required).
- To turn off their mobile phones.
- The confidentiality agreement.
- Time at the end of the meeting will be allotted for questions.

19.10 Ice-breaker.
19.20 Opening – Ground, protect and raise energies.

Part One – Connecting with the higher beings
19.25 Give information about the higher beings.
19.35 Visualisation to meet the higher beings, feel their energies and receive a message from them.
19.50 Students share and give feedback from the visualisation.
Additional activities for part one – spiritual cards of the higher beings, writing to the higher beings.

<u>Part Two – How the higher beings can help us</u>
20.00 Give information about how the higher beings can help us.
20.05 Activity to ask the higher beings for help for yourself in pairs or threes, depending on numbers.
20.20 Short healing session in pairs, taking it in turns to ask the higher beings for their healing energy, and then share their experiences with each other.
Additional activities and visualisations for part two – activity to ask the higher beings to help somebody else, visualisation for the higher beings to work on your participants' auras to give protection.

20.45 Questions.
20.55 Closing. Protect, make personal energies safe and ground.
21.00 Finish – Could have hot drinks and a chat afterwards.

A half-day programme of 3 hours for an introduction to spirituality
For adult beginners.
Positive statement: My course helps my participants to understand the spiritual realms and connect easily with their spirits and guides.
Meet at 9.15 for a 9.30 start. Hand out name tags, give participants a hot drink, get people talking or let each person draw a spiritual card and say why they feel they have chosen this card.
9.30 Welcome talk to tell the participants:
- The main topics – Incarnation and life's lessons, Evolving, Spirits and guides.
- What they should get out of the meeting.
- Times and length of breaks and the finish time.
- Where the toilets are.

- The fire procedures (if required).
- To turn off their mobile phones.
- The confidentiality agreement.
- Details of any items you may have for sale.
- Time at the end of the meeting will be allotted for questions.

9.40 Ice-breaker.

9.50 Opening – Ground, protect and raise energies, including a brief explanation about visualisation, because, being beginners, they may not have experienced a guided visualisation before.

Part One – Incarnation and life's lessons
10.00 Information about incarnation and the task we incarnate to accomplish.
10.15 Activity in pairs to talk to partners about their possible life task.
10.25 Information about life's lessons.
10.30 Activity to make an insight book (decorate a plain notebook you give them) for participants to write their thoughts and feelings about events on a daily basis.
Additional activities for part one – with a different partner to the previous activity, discuss challenges they may have had and talk about how they can act differently next time a situation presents itself.

10.45 Break.

Part Two – Evolving
10.55 Information about how we evolve by raising our energy levels and a brief explanation about subtle energies.
11.05 Activities for participants to first sense their own aura and then that of a partner.
Additional activity for part two – spiritual cards.

<u>Part Three – Spirits and guides</u>
11.20 Information about spirits and guides.
11.30 Visualisation to meet a spirit or their guide, connect with them and ask them their name.
11.50 Draw their spirit or guide from their visualisation. If they did not see their spirit or guide, ask them to draw the energy they sensed or anything else they received in the visualisation.
12.05 Share drawings and events from the visualisation. Additional activities for part three – asking the spirits or guides for help.

12.15 Questions.
12.20 Singing a spiritual song.
12.25 Closing. Protect, make personal energies safe and ground.
12.30 Finish.

A day programme of 6 hours to meet some higher beings

For adults who are already on their spiritual path.
Positive statement: My participants make an excellent connection with the higher beings which lasts for life.
Meet at 9.45 for a 10.00 start. Hand out name tags, give participants a hot drink and allow them to chat or draw a spiritual card and say why they feel they have chosen this card.
10.00 Welcome talk to tell the participants:
- The main topics – Connecting with the higher beings, How the higher beings can help us, Personal higher beings, The higher beings' evolution and how they connect with other higher beings.
- What they should get out of the meeting.
- Times and length of breaks, lunch and the finish time.

- Where the toilets are.
- Lunch facilities, if any.
- The fire procedures (if required).
- To turn off their mobile phones.
- The confidentiality agreement.
- Details of any items you may have for sale.
- Questions will be answered during the meeting.

10.10 Ice-breaker.

10.20 Opening – Ground, protect and raise energies.

10.25 Ask the participants to write down what they expect to get out of the course and share this with the group. Ask them to keep the paper handy so that it can be reviewed at the end of the day.

Part One – Connecting with the higher beings

10.35 Information about the higher beings.

10.50 Activity to bring in and sense the energy of the higher beings with colour or sound, and then share the experiences.

11.05 Visualisation to meet and connect with the higher beings.

11.20 Break.

11.35 Draw something from the visualisation and share feedback (taking it in turns).

Additional activities for part one – spiritual cards of the higher beings.

Part Two – How the higher beings can help us

11.55 Information about the different ways the higher beings help us.

12.00 Activity to ask the higher beings for help for themselves.

12.15 Activity to ask the higher beings for help for others.

Additional activities and visualisations for part two – asking the higher beings to put their energy into an object which can be taken away and left in a specific place to radiate its energy out to help the participants or others, visualisation to ask the higher beings for help with a current issue in the news.

12.25 Close for lunch – protect, make personal energies safe and ground.
12.30 Lunch.
13.00 Open after lunch – ground, protect and raise energies.

Part Three – Personal higher beings
13.05 Activity – object drawing, making sure one of the objects is a higher being.
13.20 Feedback and sharing from object drawing.
13.35 Information about personal higher beings, e.g. spirit guides or guardian angels.
13.45 Visualisation to meet their personal higher being, communicate with them and receive a message or gift.
14.00 Sharing experiences from the visualisation.
14.10 Writing to their personal higher being with sharing, but only if they wish to give it.
Additional activities for part three – asking their higher being to stroke their aura and sense this happening, thank-you list of all the things the higher being does to help.

14.25 Break.

Part Four – The higher beings' evolution and how they connect with other higher beings
14.40 Information about the evolution of the higher beings.

14.50 Open discussion activity about how the higher beings' evolution differs from our evolution and the differences in energy vibrations.

15.05 Information about their connections with other higher beings.

15.15 Visualisation to sense the energies and signs of the other higher beings.

15.25 Sharing results of the visualisation.

Additional activities for part four – drawing a scene from the visualisation, dancing with the higher beings.

15.35 Look at the paper about expectations for the course that the participants wrote at the beginning of the day and discuss their personal outcome (taking it in turns).

15.45 Sing a song connected with the higher beings.

15.55 Closing. Protect, make personal energies safe and ground.

16.00 Finish.

A day programme of 6 hours for healing
For adults who are interested in healing friends and family.

Positive statement: My participants have the knowledge and confidence to freely give healing to others as well as themselves.

Meet at 9.45 for a 10.00 start. Hand out name tags, give participants a hot drink, get people talking or let each person draw a spiritual card and say why they feel they have chosen this card.

10.00 Welcome talk to tell the participants:
- The main topics – Our energy systems, What healing is and how to do it, Distance healing, Self-healing.
- What they should get out of the meeting.

- Times and length of breaks, lunch and the finish time.
- Where the toilets are.
- Lunch facilities, if any.
- The fire procedures (if required).
- To turn off their mobile phones.
- The confidentiality agreement.
- Details of any items you may have for sale.
- Time at the end of the meeting will be allotted for questions.

10.10 Ice-breaker.
10.20 Opening – Ground, protect and raise energies.

Part One – Our energy systems
10.25 Information about auras.
10.35 Activities to feel their own aura and then that of a partner.
10.50 Information about chakras.
11.00 Activity in pairs to sense chakras with a different partner to the previous activity.
Additional activities for part one – drawing auras, going outside and perceiving auras of trees and plants, dowsing auras or chakras.

11.20 Break.

Part Two – What healing is and how to do it
11.30 Information about healing and how it should be done and answer questions about it before they do it for themselves in the afternoon.

11.55 Close for lunch – protect, make personal energies safe and ground.

12.00 Lunch.

12.30 Open after lunch – ground, protect and raise energies.

12.35 Healing in pairs – the first partner gives an hour of healing on the second partner, with discussion and feedback between them.

13.40 Break.

13.50 Healing in pairs – the second partner gives an hour of healing on the first partner, with discussion and feedback between them.
Additional activities for part two – balancing chakras with a different partner.

14.55 Break.

Part Three – Distance healing
15.05 Information about distance-healing.
15.15 Sending distance healing to somebody the participants know.
Additional activities for part three – sending distance healing as a group to somewhere in the world that needs it.

Part Four – Self-healing
15.25 Information about self-healing.
15.30 A self-healing treatment.
Additional activity for part four – thank-you-for-health list.

15.40 Questions.
15.50 Singing or dancing to a well-known song with spiritual lyrics.
15.55 Closing. Protect, make personal energies safe and ground.
16.00 Finish.

CHAPTER EIGHT

ORGANISATION AND ADMINISTRATION

By the end of Chapter Eight you will:

- Know how to organise and promote meetings or courses
- Understand what administration should be done to run meetings and courses

Organising a Meeting or Course

You should start to organise your meeting or course at least eight weeks before it is due to run. You first need to create a programme, as explained in Chapter Seven, so you will have a title for your meeting, have identified the people you want to attract and know how long and when you want it to run.

If you are hiring a venue, look at some suitable places and book one. You will probably need to pay a deposit. You must also arrange the final payment as well as when and where you will be collecting the keys and returning them. You should find out what facilities and equipment you can use, e.g. tables, chairs, flip chart stand, kitchen, kettle, cups.

Next, decide when your participants will pay you for the meeting. Do they pay in advance, on the day or pay a deposit with the remainder due on the day? In practice, if you want to have an idea of numbers for your meeting, it is best to ask for the full amount or a deposit before the meeting, because some people say they will come and then not turn up if they have not had to part with some money beforehand.

Now choose how your participants will pay you. Will you accept cash, cheques or PayPal? Unless your meeting is extremely large or you have another business, it will not be worth investing in a credit or debit card machine to take telephone and online bookings. However, if you have a website, you can direct people to pay with a card via PayPal using the PayPal 'Pay Now' buttons. PayPal will charge you a small fee for each payment into the account. To do this you will need to sign up online for a PayPal account and link it to your bank account so that you can withdraw funds from PayPal to your bank.

You will need to decide how much you are going to charge. Apart from the obvious costs of the hire of the venue and the material things such as flip charts, paper, pens, music, tea, coffee, printing, telephone calls etc., it is about having your personal energy input being exchanged for money. Think about how much time you will be spending on your meeting with preparation, typing notes or manuals, telephone calls, emails, letters, advertising, your time during the meeting, tidying up and reflection afterwards. It can be amazing how long it all takes.

To help find the right price, look around and see what others are charging for similar meetings or courses in your area, as this can vary enormously depending on the economic conditions of your locality. By doing this you can make sure that your price is competitive. If you set your price too low, people will think that your meeting is inferior and they will not value your work, but if you set it too high, people may not be able to afford it or will expect something fantastic. However, in order to promote your meeting once you have fixed your price, you may like to offer a discount. For example, a reduction if a second meeting is booked and paid for.

Promotion

As long as there is a need for your meeting or course in your area, promotion should be a matter of letting people know your meeting or course is there. To promote your meeting or course: first, consider what your participants really want; and second, think about something special and different that you have to offer, combine the two and promote them. For example, connecting with specific higher beings which will be with them for life or giving them something physical to take away with them. If you are not holding a regular weekly or monthly meeting, you may like to consider having more than one meeting or course with continuity or a theme, so that when participants attend the first one, there will be another that they can attend at a later date. If you are doing this, you need to reflect this in the titles for your meetings, e.g. the first course could be called 'Introduction to Higher Beings' and the second one 'Advanced Higher Beings'.

Leaflets and/or cards are helpful to promote yourself locally, but you will need to produce them well in advance. If you are computer literate you can make these yourself. For this, you will need some high-quality paper or card and a good printer. Alternatively, you can get some printed from a printing service, which can look more professional, but you must be sure that they are what you want before hundreds are printed. Also, if you do not distribute all of them, you could be left with a pile of out-of-date leaflets. There are some inexpensive card printing services on the Internet, while local printers are generally more costly.

To design a leaflet or card, have a look at ones that have been produced by others to see what catches your eye and what colours, fonts and pictures you like. People like to look at pictures, so try to include more pictures than words.

Items to think about including in your leaflet are:

- Your name and your business name, if you have one.
- Meeting or course title.
- Details of your meeting or course and what your participants will get out of it.
- Your contact details – telephone number (you may want to include times they can contact you to avoid being available 24/7); website address, if you have one; email address; and the address where the meeting is being held.
- Details of your spiritual experience and brief details about yourself.
- Price of the meeting.
- When you have run a number of meetings and courses you may like to include some favourable comments from previous participants.

When you have finished designing your leaflet, let a good friend read it and give you their honest feedback.

To follow are some types of promotion, some of which require technical experience which is beyond the scope of this book. If a particular skill is required, then specialists in their field, courses or books should be consulted.

Word of mouth is free and one of the best types of promotion. Many people rely heavily on advice from friends and family and take notice of what they say, so talk enthusiastically to as many people as you can about your meeting or course. Always have some leaflets or cards on you to give to people you meet and, if they are enthusiastic, provide them with some to give to others.

Websites are great for promoting meetings and courses. There are a number of free or cheap website building programmes; however, if you use one of these, make sure that it looks as professional as possible with no spelling or other glaring mistakes. You could invest in having one created, but it can be an expensive option.

Social networking is relatively new and another good form of promotion. It includes services such as Facebook, Twitter, LinkedIn, YouTube and Flickr. These networking communities are free, but be mindful of the time consumed using them. If doing this, try to keep your business separate from your private life, so, for example, with Facebook, have separate pages for private and business use.

An emailing list can be built up over time with people who you feel would be interested; people who have enquired about your meetings and previous attendees. This list can be built up as a separate group of contacts in your email account, but be careful that you do not lose it if you change your email address or account. When you organise a new meeting or course, you can compose just one email and send it to everyone in your group list. You could also extend this further by sending a newsletter out every month or three months, giving spiritual information and details of your next meetings or courses.

Advertising in newspapers and magazines can be used to promote your meeting or course, but it is often costly and may not produce the results you had hoped for. If, or when, you advertise, be clear about where it is being placed, who will see it and how many will see it. Be clear about what actions people have to take when they reply to your advertisement, e.g. phone, visit, email.

Also, with advertisements in magazines, you will probably receive telephone calls from other magazines wanting you to advertise in their publication. Some of these sales people can be extremely persistent, even if you say you are not interested.

Writing articles for newspapers and magazines can be a cost-effective way to gain publicity. Editors are always looking for new items for their columns and will favour pieces that are already typed and of good quality so that they can add them to their publication without spending time on them. Think of something that you do that will make news, such as your brand-new venture, having an unusual course or venue etc. If your first article does not get published, the editor may have thought that there was a more interesting piece of news for that publication, so try sending another article for a different issue.

Talks are another good way to gain promotion for your meetings and courses. There are many groups and organisations that are looking for speakers for their meetings. Try not to be daunted at the prospect of giving a talk, as the more you do the more confidence you will gain and the easier it becomes. You may receive a little money for the talk, but, at the very least, your expenses should be reimbursed. When you give a talk, make sure that you take plenty of leaflets to hand out.

Local or hospital radio interviews can also give promotion. If you do this, thoroughly prepare your talk before you go and remember that local radio stations often need two to five minute slots filled at short notice, so be ready for this by having something prepared before you contact them.

Networking can be done by leaving leaflets or putting up posters in health food shops, new age shops etc. Put up postcard-size leaflets on ad boards in newsagents, small post offices and local shops. Get to know shop owners so that you can promote yourself with a poster or leaflets in their shop. You could put flyers on boards in supermarkets, video shops, laundrettes, libraries etc., but get the permission of the establishment concerned. Some libraries will allow leaflets for profit-making events, but most will only promote non-profit making ones.

If you are creating posters you can make them yourself on a computer, although you can have some professionally produced, but these will be expensive. You should make sure they are colourful with big pictures and large, but not much, writing. So limit the information to your meeting or course title, a brief sentence describing it, the date and times, the venue and its address, contact name, website address, e-mail address or telephone number and the cost. When you have produced it, put it up on a wall, stand well back and look at it. What you observe is what other people will see. What catches your eye first? Is it easy to read? Is it clearly set out? Are the colours right? Have you got your message across? Have you included a way for people to contact you?

Gift vouchers can be created to help you gain more attendees, because people are often stuck for a present for a friend or relative, so promote them on your website and in your leaflets.

Positive thoughts about your meeting or course help enormously, because every thought or visualisation that we have, impresses its energy onto our subconscious mind and into our aura, which affects how we feel, our outlook and our future.

Higher beings will also help with promotion, if asked, as well as visualising and affirming for a great, well-attended meeting.

Administration

When somebody books a meeting, you must acknowledge this with an email or letter confirming their booking and providing the following information: meeting date, start and finish times, title of the course, details of how to find the venue, lunch arrangements (if it is a day course) and anything else you would like them to bring or do beforehand.

An example of a booking confirmation letter:

Your name or business name
Your address
Your telephone number, web and email address

Date

Attendee's address

Dear attendee's name,
Thank you for your £15.00 PayPal deposit for the Lemurian Planetary Healing Day. I have pleasure in confirming your booking on Saturday 29th June. The remainder of £30 is due on the day.

The day will run from 10.00 to 16.00 and is at Hampton Village Hall, River Street, Hampton, Wessex WX12 3AB. I will provide an assortment of hot drinks, filtered water and biscuits, but please bring a packed lunch. I am enclosing directions.

If you have any questions about the day, please contact me; otherwise I am really looking forward to meeting you at the end of June.

With love and light

Your name

It is handy to have directions with a Google map of how to get to your venue stored on your computer, so that you can attach them to an email or print them to enclose with a letter. Additionally, some people may travel a long way and require accommodation. So make some enquiries with people who run local bed and breakfast facilities and compile a list to send out, if required.

When sending emails and letters, as well as other information, you must be aware of how you present yourself. So make sure there are no spelling or grammatical errors and that all correspondence looks professional and genuinely reflects you and your energy. Also, make sure that your stationery and envelopes are a good quality and match.

For people who booked a while in advance, it is also helpful to send an email to remind them three days to a week before your meeting or course is due and reiterate your booking confirmation letter.

General Administration

If you receive payment for your meetings and courses then you should consider having public liability insurance. This is in case somebody hurts themselves while at your meeting and in your care. In the UK, this insurance is usually in the region of £100 per year for £2,000,000 of cover. There are a number of insurance companies that can be found on the Internet that will give you a quote.

Regarding finances, you will need to keep records of all your income and expenditure from meetings and courses. This can be a book with income on a left-hand page and expenditure on the opposite page. With the income page, the column listings are usually date, participants' name, meeting attended and payment received. With column listings for expenditure, they are usually date, name of person or company, what the item is and amount paid. When it comes to expenditure, make sure that you keep receipts for everything, which will include things such as venue hire, stationery, printer ink cartridges, insurance, advertising, telephone costs (or an appropriate percentage of your home or mobile phone bill). At the end of the meeting or month, and at the end of your financial year, you can total the two sides and subtract the expenditure from the income, which will give you your profit. If you can use computer spreadsheets it will be easier, as the spreadsheet will do the maths.

The following are examples of an accounting book for a Beginners Spiritual Course which was run on 30th July. Needless to say, it is all fictitious, including the names.

INCOME

Date	Name	Course	Amount
4th July	Jane Jones	Beginners Spiritual Deposit	10.00
6th July	Mr & Mrs N Harry	Beginners Spiritual Depositx2	20.00
9th July	Julia Netherby	Beginners Spiritual Course	40.00
12th July	Tim Douglas	Beginners Spiritual Deposit	10.00
22nd July	Tim & Val Hay	Beginners Spiritual Depositx2	20.00
23rd July	Sara Webb	Beginners Spiritual Deposit	10.00
28th July	Sheena Bow	Beginners Spiritual Course	40.00
30th July	Jane Jones	Beginners Spiritual Remainder	30.00
30th July	Mr & Mrs N Harry	Beginners Spiritual Remainderx2	60.00
30th July	Tim Douglas	Beginners Spiritual Remainder	30.00
30th July	Tim & Val Hay	Beginners Spiritual Remainderx2	60.00
30th July	Sara Webb	Beginners Spiritual Remainder	30.00
			360.00

EXPENDITURE

Date	Name	Details	Amount
21st June	Stickle Village Hall	Hire of hall for 30th July	60.00
22nd June	Happy Computing	Website domain name	3.99
22nd June	Shuggles Insurance	Public Liability Insurance	91.20
22nd June	Hippy Stationers	Paper, Envelopes & Stamps	13.56
23rd June	K Phones	Mobile Phone Top Up	20.00
30th June	Hippy Stationers	Flipcharts, easel and pens	34.16
30th June	The Music Shop	CD for course	9.99
24th July	Hippy Stationers	Crayons & 15 clip boards	42.30
24th July	Jim's Stores	Candles	6.21
29th July	Jim's Stores	Tea, coffee, milk & biscuits	15.69
			297.10

This account depicts somebody running their first course. The expenditure of £297.10 is taken away from the income of £360.00 to give a profit of £62.90. This includes start-up costs of £171.65 for website domain name, insurance, flipcharts, easel, pens, crayons and clip boards.

The accounts can be totalled on a monthly basis or for each course, as in the example above. So a couple of facing pages are used for each month or course and a couple of further pages for the next month or course.

If you are not good at maths or your books get too complicated for you to manage, you can hire the services of an accountant. The accountant will also fill in your tax return and deal with HM Revenue & Customs on your behalf. Whether you employ the services of an accountant or not, you will need to keep a record of your income, all receipts from business-related purchases, bank statements, card receipts and cheque book stubs.

It is also advisable to open a separate business bank account, so that your business money does not get mixed with your private money. If you shop around, it is possible to obtain a business bank account which does not charge fees to small businesses for the first few months.

Also, in the UK, by law you must inform HM Revenue & Customs that you have self-employed income, even if you have another job and you are running courses part time. Go to www.hmrc.gov.uk or write to them at the address given in your most recent correspondence with them. They also offer advice and information for new businesses. The income tax year in the UK runs from 6th April to 5th April the following year. However, your self-employed accounting year can run from any date, as long as it is the same date each year, unless it is your first year of trading, when it can be longer.

You will also have to pay Class 2 National Insurance. This is a set amount that must be paid by self-employed people each week and can be paid by direct debit monthly in arrears or every six months in January and July. You will also need to pay Class 4 National Insurance on your profit if it exceeds the lower limit. This is worked out on your tax return and paid with your income tax.

You may also like to think about putting money aside for a personal pension. If you do this, you will get tax relief on your payments. You will need to shop around for the best pension for you and discuss it with financial experts.

Conclusion

I hope you are now filled with the confidence and enthusiasm, as well as knowledge, to help you run your own meetings and courses. I wish you great success with your endeavours.

With love and blessings

Margaret Merrison

ALSO BY MARGARET MERRISON

Both titles are available in paperback and on Amazon Kindle.

TRUE BEING: A BEGINNER'S GUIDE TO FINDING, WALKING AND ENJOYING YOUR SPIRITUAL PATH

True Being is a user-friendly book that you will turn to again and again for inspiration on your journey of spiritual discovery! You will connect with spirit guides, angels and ascended masters and develop your own unique spirituality in a safe, grounded and protected way. You will learn how to find your life path and realise who you really are and why you are here now. There are many activities and visualisations spread throughout *True Being* to help you experience the energies and consolidate the information, as well as a number of stories that will help you to bring the spiritual realms into your world of everyday living. *True Being* is also a comprehensive guide for people leading spiritual groups or circles because, as well as the information, there are activities and visualisations for each subject that can easily be incorporated into group sessions.

WHAT ARE UNICORNS?

This concise book about unicorns will answer your questions about these great, playful, pure beings from the higher realms, as well as giving you more unicorn information than you can imagine. *What Are Unicorns?* will help you to raise and purify your vibrations, so you can easily connect with the wonderful natural energy of the unicorns in a safe way. If you are interested in unicorns and want to learn how to experience their magnificent energy, *What Are Unicorns?* is the book for you.

Lightning Source UK Ltd.
Milton Keynes UK
UKHW021128180521
383928UK00006B/1385